CONTENTS

Readings From the United States

Readings From Around the World

from *The Mountains of California*
by John Muir

In the 1800's, Scottish naturalist John Muir walked across much of the United States making observations, taking notes, and describing the natural life found in each region. Muir wrote extensively about his observations of nature and stressed the importance of conservation. He launched a campaign urging the federal government to adopt a forest conservation policy. Through his efforts, Sequoia and Yosemite national parks were established in 1890. In 1892, Muir founded the Sierra Club, which began a national conservation movement. This excerpt about the Sierra Nevada is from Muir's book, *The Mountains of California,* published in 1894.

Making your way through the mazes of the Coast Range to the summit of any of the inner peaks or passes opposite San Francisco, in the clear springtime, the grandest and most telling of all California landscapes is outspread before you. At your feet lies the great Central Valley glowing golden in the sunshine, extending north and south farther than the eye can reach, one smooth, flowery, lake-like bed of fertile soil. Along its eastern margin rises the mighty Sierra, miles in height, reposing like a smooth, cumulous cloud in the sunny sky, and so gloriously colored, and so luminous, it seems to be not clothed with light, but wholly composed of it, like the wall of some celestial city. Along the top, and extending a good way down, you see a pale, pearl gray belt of snow; and below it a belt of blue and dark purple, marking the extension of the forests; and along the base of the range a broad belt of rose purple and yellow, where lie the miner's goldfields and the foot-hill gardens. All these colored belts blending smoothly make a wall of light ineffably fine, and as beautiful as a rainbow, yet firm as adamant.

When I first enjoyed this superb view, one glowing April day, from the summit of the Pacheco Pass, the Central Valley, but little trampled or plowed as yet, was one furred, rich sheet of golden composite, and the luminous wall of the mountains shone in all its glory. Then it seemed to me the Sierra should be called not the Nevada, or Snowy Range, but the Range of Light. And after ten years spent in the heart of it, rejoicing and wondering, bathing in its glorious floods of light, seeing the sunbursts of morning among the ivy peaks, the noonday radiance on the trees and rocks and snow, the flush of the alpenglow, and a thousand dashing waterfalls with their marvelous abundance of irised spray, it still seems to me above all others the Range of Light, the most divinely beautiful of all the mountain-chains I have ever seen.

The Sierra is about 500 miles long, 70 miles wide, and from 7,000 to nearly 15,000 feet high. In general views no mark of man is visible on it, nor anything to suggest the richness of the life it cherishes, or the depth and grandeur of its sculpture. None of its magnificent forest-crowned ridges rises much above the general level to publish its wealth. No great valley or lake is seen, or river, or group of well-marked features of any kind, standing out in distinct pictures. Even the summit-peaks, so clear and high in the sky, seem comparatively smooth and featureless. Nevertheless, glaciers are still at work in the shadows of the peaks, and thousands of lakes and meadows shine and bloom beneath them, and the whole range is furrowed with canyons to a depth of from 2,000 to 5,000 feet, in which once flowed majestic glaciers, and in which now flow and sing a band of beautiful rivers.

reposing   resting
luminous   full of light
celestial   relating to the sky or heavens

ineffably   indescribably
adamant   a hard precious stone
composite   a mixture of different plants

Though of such stupendous depth, these famous canyons are not raw, gloomy, jagged-walled gorges, savage and inaccessible. With rough passages here and there they still make delightful pathways for the mountaineer, conducting from the fertile lowlands to the highest icy fountains, as a kind of mountain streets full of charming life and light, graded and sculptured by the ancient glaciers, and presenting, throughout all their courses, a rich variety of novel and attractive scenery, the most attractive that has yet been discovered in the mountain-ranges of the world.

In many places, especially in the middle region of the western flank of the range, the main canyons widen into spacious valleys or parks, diversified like artificial landscape-gardens, with charming groves and meadows, and thickets of blooming bushes, while the lofty, retiring walls, infinitely varied in form and sculpture, are fringed with ferns, flowering plants of many species, oaks, and evergreens, which find anchorage on a thousands narrow steps and benches; while the whole is enlivened and made glorious with rejoicing streams that come dancing and foaming over the sunny brows of the cliffs to join the shining river that flows in tranquil beauty down the middle of each one of them.

The walls of these park valleys of the Yosemite kind are made up of rocks mountains in size, partly separated from each other by narrow gorges and side-canyons; and they are so sheer in front, and so compactly built together on a level floor, that, comprehensively seen, the parks they inclose look like immense halls and temples lighted from above. Every rock seems to glow with life. Some lean back in majestic repose; others, absolutely sheer, or nearly so, for thousands of feet, advance their brows in thoughtful attitudes beyond their companions, giving welcome to storms and calms alike, seemingly conscious yet heedless of everything going on about them, awful in stern majesty... yet associated with beauty of the frailest and most fleeting forms; their feet set in pine groves and gay emerald meadows, their brows in the sky; bathed in light, bathed in floods of singing water, while snow-clouds, avalanches, and the winds shine and surge and wreathe about them as they years go by, as if into these mountain mansions Nature had taken pains to gather their choicest treasures.

inaccessible   not able to be reached
diversified   a variety of
infinitely   endlessly
anchorage   a means of securing

comprehensively   completely
avalanches   large masses of snow, ice, and rocks
sliding swiftly down a mountain

Think It Over

1. Why is Muir's description of the Sierra Nevada an authentic historical document?

2. What facts does Muir include here that could not have come from his own personal observations?

Name _____ Date _____

"America the Beautiful"
by Katharine Lee Bates

Katharine Lee Bates was an English professor at Wellesley College in Massachusetts. She wrote many poems and children's books during her long career. However, she is best known for writing the words to "America the Beautiful." Bates wrote the hymn in 1893 and revised it in 1911. Over the years, many people have suggested that this song should become the national anthem of the United States.

O beautiful for spacious skies,
For amber waves of grain,
For purple mountain majesties
Above the fruited plain!
America! America!
God shed His grace on thee
And crown thy good with brotherhood
From sea to shining sea!

O beautiful for pilgrim feet,
Whose stern, impassioned stress
A thoroughfare for freedom beat
Across the wilderness!
America! America!
God mend thine every flaw,
Confirm thy soul in self-control,
Thy liberty in law!

O beautiful for heroes proved
In liberating strife,
Who more than self their country loved,
And mercy more than life!
America! America!
May God thy gold refine,
Till all success be nobleness
And every gain divine!

O beautiful for patriot dream
That sees beyond the years
Thine alabaster cities gleam
Undimmed by human tears!
America! America!
God shed his grace on thee,
And crown thy good with brotherhood
From sea to shining sea!

amber   brownish yellow color
strife   the act or condition of fighting or quarreling; conflict

alabaster   of highly polished white stone

Think It Over

1. Patriotic songs are meant to stir feelings of pride in one's country. How does the first verse of "America the Beautiful" encourage feelings of pride?

2. Why do you think Bates included the words "crown thy good with brotherhood"?

"The Spider Woman"
Navajo Tale

The following folk tale tells how Navajo women learned to weave. Weaving is an important part of Navajo culture. The Kisani woman, the main character, is rejected by society because she is so ugly.

Near the path up there among some rocks, she saw smoke rising up from the ground. "I wonder what that could be?" she asked herself, and decided to go there in search of food and warmth. To her surprise, when she reached her destination she found that the smoke was rising from the bottom of a little round hole. Waving the smoke away, she was able to look inside the hole. And much to her amazement she saw a strange looking old woman who was every bit as ugly as she was sitting by the warmth of the fire spinning a web. It was the Spider Woman, and when she saw a shadow over the hole she looked up and saw the Kisani woman staring down at her.

"Do not be afraid, my daughter. Come down into my house and visit with me," the old woman said.

"The hole is much too small for me to enter," replied the Kisani woman.

"It is big enough," replied the Spider Woman.

Then she blew her breath up the hole four times and it opened out bigger and bigger until it became a wide passageway, with four ladders leading up to the top. On the east was a white ladder, on the south a blue one, on the west a yellow one, and on the north a black one.

The Kisani woman climbed down the blue ladder into the abode of the Spider Woman who was weaving something. "Come down and sit here beside me and watch what I do, my grandchild," the old woman said. And the Kisani woman did as she asked.

The Spider Woman was using a stick about a foot long with a hole in one end like a needle, and with this she passed the thread in and out, making a blanket. "What is this that you do, grandmother?" the Kisani girl asked.

"It is a blanket I weave," the old woman replied.

"Does it have a name, my grandmother?"

"I will name it Black Design Blanket." And this became the Black Design Blanket, the first blanket of the Navajo. . . . Then Spider Woman told the girl the sun was low and it would soon be dark. . . .

"It is late and I must be leaving," the girl said.

"Please. Spend the night with me, my grandchild." This the Kisani woman agreed to and began to settle for the night. . . .

Spider Woman made some dumplings out of grass seeds and fed the girl and the next morning started weaving another blanket. She worked so fast that she finished it that day. It was square and as long as her arm and she named this new blanket Pretty Design Blanket. The girl watched her all day and stayed there a second night, and the following morning the Spider Woman started still another blanket. She finished this blanket, which she called White Striped Blanket, that day, and on the fourth morning she began another. This was a "Beautiful Design Skirt" such as Yeibichai dancers and Snake dancers wear, and was white with figures in black.

The next morning the Kisani girl went back to the hogan where she had been staying and asked the Navajos for some cotton in three colors—yellow, black, and white. After the cotton had been given to her, she put up a loom, but not like the Spider Woman's loom. She put it up the way Navajo women do now and began a blanket. Her blanket was about half done when another Kisani woman came in and

abode home

hogan a traditional, earth-covered Navajo house

looked at the loom and the design. The girl had made a picture of a bird on both sides of the blanket.

"Where did you learn to do that?" the Kisani woman asked. "I did this on my own thought," answered the girl. "It is called a Black Design Blanket."

She finished it in one day, and the next morning she put up her loom again and asked for more cotton to weave. She made a Beautiful Design Skirt the same day. It was finished when two Kisani men came to see what she was doing and asked to see the blankets she had made. One examined the Beautiful Design Blanket very carefully. The second man observed the Black Design weaving. They then returned to their homes and made looms, copying the designs they had learned. And this is why it is the Kisani men who are known for their beautiful weaving.

The girl only made two blankets and then went back to Spider Woman's house. Spider Woman was now weaving a wicker water jar and after that she wove a big carrying basket such as Navajo women used to carry on their backs. The Kisani girl learned to make the basket and then the water jar. "When I went back," she told Spider Woman, "I showed the people how to make blankets like yours. Now

loom   an apparatus for making thread or yarn into cloth by weaving strands together

I will go back and make carrying baskets and water jars."

"That is good," said Spider Woman. "I am glad you have taught them. But whenever you make a blanket, you must leave a hole in the middle the way I do. For if you do not, your weaving thoughts will be trapped within the cotton and not only will it bring you bad luck, but it will drive you mad."

The girl went back to her hogan and made a carrying basket and a water jar.

"Where do you learn all these things?" The People* asked.

"I just guessed it out," she said.

The Navajo women watched her, and soon they were all making carrying baskets and then they learned to make water jars and blankets too, just like those of the Spider Woman. Unlike the Kisani men, it is the Navajo women who kept on with their blanket weaving. And they always left the spider-hole in the center of a spider web. That keeps them from getting "blanket sickness" of the mind from keeping the weaving patterns inside their heads. Navajo women almost never draw their blanket patterns down but keep them inside as Spider Woman did.

And that's true, even today.

_____

* "The People" is how the Navajo refer to themselves.

Think It Over

1. "Spider Woman" was first told in the Navajo language. Also, like many folk tales, the story was passed on orally for generations before it was ever written down. How might these two facts affect the authenticity of this version of the story?

Two Descriptions of the Middle Passage
from *Black Cargoes* by David P. Mannix

Enslaved Africans were packed onto ships and brought to the Americas on a route known as the Middle Passage. The following two excerpts are the views and observations of men who witnessed it firsthand. John Newton was a former slave ship captain who later became a minister. Dr. Falconbridge was a surgeon who served on a slave ship during the time of the African slave trade.

The Reverend John Newton:

The cargo of a vessel of a hundred tons or a little more is calculated to purchase from 220 to 250 slaves. Their lodging rooms below the deck which are three (for the men, the boys, and the women) besides a place for the sick, are sometimes more than five feet high and sometimes less; and this height is divided toward the middle for the slaves lie in two rows, one above the other, on each side of the ship, close to each other like books upon a shelf. I have known them so close that the shelf would not easily contain one more.

The poor creatures, thus cramped, are likewise in irons for the most part which makes it difficult for them to turn or move or attempt to rise or to lie down without hurting themselves or each other. Every morning, perhaps, more instances than one are found of the living and the dead fastened together.

ensued   took place

Dr. Falconbridge:

Some wet and blowing weather . . . having occasioned the port-holes to be shut and the grating to be covered, . . . fever among the Negroes ensued. While they were in this situation, I frequently went down among them till at length their rooms became so extremely hot as to be only bearable for a very short time. . . . The climate was too warm to admit the wearing of any clothing but a shirt and that I had pulled off before I went down; notwithstanding which, by only continuing among them for about a quarter of an hour, I was so overcome with the heat, stench and foul air that I nearly fainted; and it was only with assistance that I could get on deck. The consequence was that I soon after fell sick of the same disorder from which I did not recover for several months.

Think It Over

1. Both of these reports are by officers who worked on slave ships. Why do you think there are fewer eyewitness accounts from enslaved Africans on the Middle Passage?

2. What kind of information could an African witness give that Newton and Falconbridge could not?

from the **Mayflower Compact**

Before the *Mayflower* anchored in what is now Provincetown Harbor off Cape Cod, Massachusetts, the ship's 41 male passengers signed a binding agreement that established a basis for self-government. This agreement became known as the Mayflower Compact. Its signers promised to create a government based on the consent of the governed and ruled by law. Since women had no political rights, the women aboard the *Mayflower* were not asked to sign the Mayflower Compact.

In the name of God Amen, We whose names are underwritten, the loyal subjects of the dread sovereign Lord King James by the grace of God, of Great Britain, France, and Ireland king, defender of the faith, etc.

Having undertaken for the glory of God, and advancements of the Christian faith and honor of our King and country, a voyage to plant the first colony in the northern parts of Virginia, do by these presents solemnly and mutually in the presence of God, and one of another, covenant and combine ourselves together into a civil body politic; for our better ordering and preservation and further-

ance of the ends afore said; and by virtue hereof to enact, constitute, and frame such just and equal laws, ordinances, acts, constitutions, and offices, from time to time, as shall be thought most meet and convenient for the general good of the colony: unto which we promise all due submission and obedience.

In witness whereof we have here under subscribed our names at Cape Cod the 11 of November, in the year the reign of our sovereign Lord King James of England, France, and Ireland, the eighteenth and of Scotland the fifty-fourth Anno Domini 1620.

sovereign   ruler; king
covenant   enter into an agreement

Think It Over

1. Pilgrim men signed the Mayflower Compact while they were still on board ship. What can the document tell us about the government of the Plymouth colony? What can it not tell us?

"How I Became a Printer"
by Benjamin Franklin

This excerpt from Benjamin Franklin's autobiography describes his early education and his apprenticeship to his brother James, a Boston printer. Franklin also writes about the role printers played in bringing attention to colonial opposition to British rule.

I was put to the grammar-school at eight years of age, my father intending to devote me, as the tithe of his sons, to the service of the Church. My early readiness in learning to read (which must have been very early, as I do not remember when I could not read), and the opinion of all his friends, that I should certainly make a good scholar, encouraged him in this purpose of his. . . . But my father, in the mean time, from the view of the expense of a college education, which having so large a family he could not well afford . . . took me from the grammar-school, and sent me to a school for writing and arithmetic. . . . At ten years old I was taken home to assist my father in his business, which was that of a tallow-chandler and soapboiler. . . . Accordingly, I was employed in cutting wick for the candles, filling the dipping mold and the molds for cast candles, attending the shop, going of errands etc.

I disliked the trade, and had a strong inclination for the sea, but my father declared against it. However, living near the water, I was much in and about it, learned early to swim well, and to manage boats; and when in a boat or canoe with other boys, I was commonly allowed to govern, especially in any case of difficulty; and upon other occasions I was generally a leader among the boys. . . .

From a child I was fond of reading, and all the little money that came into my hands was ever laid out in books. . . .

This bookish inclination at length determined my father to make me a printer, though he had already one son (James) of that profession. In 1717 my brother James returned from England with a press and letters to set up his business in Boston. I liked it much better than that of my father, but still had a hankering for the sea. To prevent the apprehended effect of such an inclination, my father was impatient to have me bound to my brother. I stood out some time, but at last was persuaded, and signed the indenture when I was yet but twelve years old. I was to serve as an apprentice till I was twenty-one years of age, only I was to be allowed journeyman's wages during the last year. In a little time I made great proficiency in the business, and became a useful hand to my brother.

Though a brother, he considered himself as my master, and me as his apprentice, and accordingly, expected the same services from me as he would from another, while I thought he demeaned me too much in some he required of me, who from a brother expected more indulgence. Our disputes were often brought before our father, and I fancy I was either generally in the right, or else a better pleader, because the judgment was generally in my favor. But my brother was passionate, and had often beaten me, which I took extremely amiss; and, thinking my apprenticeship very tedious, I was continually wishing for some opportunity of shortening it, which at length offered in a manner unexpected.

One of the pieces in our newspaper on some political point, which I have now forgotten, gave offense to the Assembly. He [James] was taken up, censured, and imprisoned for a month, by the speaker's warrant, I suppose, because he would not discover [reveal] his author. I too was taken up and examined before the council; but, though I did not give them any satisfaction, they contented themselves with admonishing

tithe   one tenth of one's annual income for support of the church

censured   criticized
admonishing   warning a person to correct some fault

me, and dismissed me, considering me, perhaps, as an apprentice, who was bound to keep his master's secrets.

During my brother's confinement, which I resented a good deal, notwithstanding our private differences, I had the management of the paper; and I made bold to give our rulers some rubs in it, which my brother took very kindly, while others began to consider me in an unfavorable light, as a young genius that had a turn for libeling and satire. My brother's discharge was accompanied with an order of the House (a very odd one), that "James Franklin should no longer print the paper called the New England Courant."

There was a consultation held in our printing-house among his friends, what he should do in this case. Some proposed to evade the order by changing the name of the paper; but my brother, seeing inconveniences in that, it was finally concluded on as a better way, to let it be printed for the future under the name of BENJAMIN FRANKLIN; and to avoid the censure of the Assembly, that might fall on him as still printing it by his apprentice, the contrivance was that my old indenture should be returned to me, with full discharge on the back of it, to be shown on occasion, but to secure to him the benefit of my service, I was to sign new indentures for the remainder of the term, which were to be kept private. A very flimsy scheme it was; however, it was immediately executed, and the paper went on accordingly, under my name for several months.

notwithstanding in spite of
satire the use of irony and humor to criticize or make fun of something bad or foolish

contrivance a plan

Think It Over

1. Benjamin Franklin wrote his autobiography when he was around 50 years old. How does an autobiography differ from a diary as a source of historical information?

2. Based on this excerpt, how do you think Benjamin Franklin viewed the British?

from *Common Sense*
by Thomas Paine

In January 1776, Patriot Thomas Paine published a pamphlet called *Common Sense*. In the following passage from that pamphlet, Paine presents several arguments for declaring independence from Britain. He also discusses representative government.

Another reason why the present time is preferable to all others, is, that the fewer our numbers are, the more land there is yet unoccupied, which instead of being lavished by the k__ on his worthless dependents, may be hereafter applied, not only to the discharge of the present debt, but to the constant support of government. No nation under heaven hath such an advantage as this.

The infant state of the colonies, as it is called, so far from being against, is an argument in favor of independence. We are sufficiently numerous, and were we more so, we might be less united. It is a matter worthy of observation, that the more a country is peopled, the smaller their armies are. In military numbers, the ancients far exceeded the moderns: and the reason is evident, for trade being the consequence of population, men become too much absorbed thereby to attend to anything else. Commerce diminishes the spirit, both of patriotism and military defense. And history sufficiently informs us, that the bravest achievements were always accomplished in the non-age of a nation. . . . The more men have to lose, the less willing are they to venture. The rich are in general slaves to fear, and submit to courtly power with the trembling duplicity of a spaniel.

Youth is the seed time of good habits, as well in nations as in individuals. It might be difficult, if not impossible, to form the continent into one government half a century hence. The vast variety of interests, occasioned by an increase in trade and population, would create confusion. Colony would be against colony. Each being able might scorn each other's assistance; and while the proud and foolish glorified in their little distinctions, the wise would lament that the union had not been formed before. . . .

The present time, likewise, is that peculiar time, which never happens to a nation but once, [that is] the time of forming itself into a government. Most nations have let slip this opportunity, and by that means have been compelled to receive laws from their conquerors, instead of making laws for themselves. First, they had a king, and then a form of government; whereas, the articles or charter for government should be formed first, and men delegated to execute them afterward: but from the errors of other nations, let us learn wisdom, and lay hold of the present opportunity—to begin government at the right end. . . .

In a former page I likewise mentioned the necessity of a large and equal representation; and there is no political matter which more deserves our attention. A small number of electors, or a small number of representatives, are equally dangerous. But if the number of representatives be not only small, but unequal, the danger is increased. . . .

Immediate necessity makes many things convenient, which if continued would grow into oppressions. Expedience and right are different things. When the calamities of America required a consultation, there was no method so ready, or at that time so proper, as to appoint persons from the several Houses of Assembly for that purpose and the wisdom with which they have proceeded hath preserved this continent from ruin. But as it is more than probable that we shall never be without a Congress, every well wisher to good order, must own, that the mode for

venture   take risks
duplicity   the practice of dealing with others in a tricky way

conquerors   people who gain control by force
expedience   the condition of being convenient or useful

choosing members of that body, deserves consideration. And I put it as a question to those who make a study of mankind, whether representation and election is not too great a power for one and the same body of men to possess? When we are planning for posterity, we ought to remember that virtue is not hereditary.

Think It Over

1. To support what particular cause did Thomas Paine write this document?

2. *Common Sense* was read and discussed throughout the 13 colonies. In evaluating a historical document, why is it important to know how popular and influential the document was?

Letters on Independence
by John Adams and Abigail Adams

John Adams and his wife, Abigail, corresponded through lengthy letters during John's many trips away from home. An avid letter writer, Abigail wrote to her family and friends about her life, including her observations of the political scene. She supported women's rights and opposed slavery. On March 31, 1776, Abigail Adams wrote to her husband while the Continental Congress discussed declaring independence. She reminded him that the legislators should "remember the ladies" when writing the new laws. John Adams responded jokingly to his wife's concerns.

Abigail to John
November 27, 1775

I wish I knew what mighty things were fabricating. If a form of government is to be established here, what one will be assumed? Will it be left to our assemblies to choose one? And will not many men have many minds? And shall we not run into dissensions among ourselves? . . .

The building up of a great empire . . . may now, I suppose, be realized even by the unbelievers. Yet, will not ten thousand difficulties arise in the formation of it? The reins of government have been so long slackened that I fear the people will not quietly submit to those restraints which are necessary for the peace and security of the community. If we separate from Britain, what code of laws will be established? How shall we be governed so as to retain our liberties? Can any government be free which is not administered by general stated laws? Who shall frame these laws? Who will give them force and energy? It is true your [the Congress's] resolutions, as a body, have hitherto had the force of laws; but will they continue to have?

When I consider these things, and the prejudices of people in favor of ancient customs and regulations, I feel anxious for the fate of our monarchy or democracy, or whatever is to take place. I soon get lost in a labyrinth of perplexities; but, whatever occurs, may justice and righteousness be

the stability of out times, and order arise out of confusion. Great difficulties may be surmounted by patience and perseverance.

Abigail to John
March 31, 1776

I long to hear that you have declared an independency—and by the way in the new code of laws which I suppose it will be necessary for you to make I desire you would remember the ladies, and be more generous and favorable to them than your ancestors. Do not put such unlimited power into the hands of the husbands. Remember all men would be tyrants if they could. If particular care and attention is not paid to the ladies we are determined to foment a rebellion, and will not hold ourselves bound by any laws in which we have no voice, or representation.

That your sex are naturally tyrannical is a truth so thoroughly established as to admit of no dispute, but such of you as wish to be happy willingly give up the harsh title of master for the more tender and endearing one of friend. Why then, not put it out of the power of the vicious and the lawless to use with cruelty and indignity with impunity. Men of sense of all ages abhor those customs which treat us only as the vassals of your sex. Regard us then as beings placed by providence under your protection and in imitation of the supreme being make use of that power only for our happiness.

fabricating   building or forming
labyrinth   a puzzle
perplexities   questions
surmounted   overcome
perseverance   continued, patient effort

tyrants   rulers having complete power; rulers who are cruel and unjust
foment   stir up; excite
impunity   freedom from being punished or harmed

John to Abigail
April 14, 1776

As to your extraordinary code of laws, I cannot but laugh. We have been told that our struggle has loosened the bands of government everywhere. That children and apprentices were disobedient—that schools and colleges were grown turbulent. . . . But your letter was the first intimation that another tribe more numerous and powerful than all the rest were grown discontented. This is rather too coarse a compliment but you are so saucy, I won't blot it out.

Depend upon it, we know better than to repeal our masculine systems. Although they are in full force, you know they are little more than theory. We dare not exert our power in its full latitude. We are obliged to go fair, and softly, and in practice you know we are the subjects. We have only the name of masters, and rather than give up this, which would completely subject us to the despotism of the petticoat, I hope General Washington, and all our brave heroes would fight. I am sure every good politician would plot, as long as he would against despotism, empire, monarchy, aristocracy, oligarchy, or ochlocracy. A fine story indeed.

despotism   dictatorship
oligarchy   a government in which a few persons hold the ruling power

ochlocracy   a government in which the masses hold the power; mob rule

Think It Over

1. How did John Adams reply to his wife's request? What does his response indicate about his thinking?

2. Abigail and John Adams wrote hundreds of letters to each other. Would reading more of their letters help you to evaluate the ones printed above? Explain.

Delegates to the Constitutional Convention
by William Pierce

William Pierce of Georgia, one of the delegates to the Constitutional Convention in 1787, wrote character sketches of some of the other delegates. His sketches include information about the age, occupation, war record, and political experience of the men who wrote the United States Constitution.

Mr. Gerry's character is marked for integrity and perseverance. He is a hesitating and laborious speaker: possesses a great degree of confidence and goes extensively into all subjects that he speaks on, without respect to elegance or flower of diction. He is connected and sometimes clear in his arguments, conceives well, and cherishes as his first virtue, a love for his country. Mr. Gerry is very much of a gentlemen in his principles and manners. He has been engaged in the mercantile line and is a man of property. He is about 37 years of age. . . .

Mr. Sherman exhibits the oddest shaped character I ever remember to have met with. He is awkward, [expressionless], and unaccountably strange in his manner. But in his train of thinking there is something regular, deep, and comprehensive; yet the oddity of his address, the vulgarisms that accompany his public speaking, and that strange New England cant which runs through his public as well as his private speaking make everything that is connected with him grotesque and laughable. And yet he deserves infinite praise,—no man has a better heart or a clearer head. If he cannot embellish he can furnish thoughts that are wise and useful. He is an able politician, and extremely artful in accomplishing any particular object. It is remarked that he seldom fails. I am told that he sits on the bench in Connecticut, and is very correct in the discharge of his judicial functions. . . . He is about 60.

Mr. Elsworth is a judge of the supreme court in Connecticut. He is a gentleman of a clear, deep, and copious understanding; eloquent, and connected in public debate; and always attentive to his duty. . . . Mr. Elsworth is about 37 years of age, a man much respected for his integrity, and venerated for his abilities.

Colonel Hamilton is deservedly celebrated for his talents. He is a practitioner of the law, and reputed to be a finished scholar. . . . Hamilton requires time to think. He inquires into every part of his subject with the searchings of philosophy, and when he comes forward he comes highly charged with interesting matter, there is no skimming over the surface of a subject with him, he must sink to the bottom to see what foundation it rests on. . . . He is about 33 years old, of small stature, and lean. . . .

Mr. Lansing is a practicing attorney at Albany, and mayor of that [city]. He has a hesitation in his speech, that will prevent his being an orator of any eminence. His legal knowledge I am told is not extensive, nor his education a good one. He is however a man of good sense, plain in his manners, and sincere in his friendships. He is about 32 years of age.

Mr. Patterson is one of those kind of men whose powers break in upon you, and create wonder and astonishment. He is a man of great modesty, with looks that bespeak talents of no great extent, but he is a classic, a lawyer, and an orator; and of a disposition so favorable to his advancement that everyone seemed ready to exalt him with their praises. He is very happy in the choice of time and manner of engaging in a debate, and never speaks but when he understands his subject well. This gentleman is about 34 years of age, of a very low stature. . . .

integrity   the quality of being honest and trustworthy; honesty
perseverance   continued, patient effort

mercantile   having to do merchants, trade, or commerce
embellish   to improve by adding something

Dr. Franklin is well known to be the greatest philosopher of the present age; all the operations of nature he seems to understand—the very heavens obey him, and the clouds yield up their lightning to be imprisoned in his rod. But what claim he has to the politician, posterity must determine. . . . He is 82 years old, and possesses an activity of mind equal to a youth of 25 years of age. . . .

Robert Morris . . . [although] not learned, yet he is as great as those who are. I am told that when he speaks in the assembly of Pennsylvania, that he bears down all before him. What could have been his reason for not speaking in the convention I know not— but he never once spoke on any point. This gentleman is about 50 years old.

Think It Over

1. What information might help you decide if William Pierce's opinions of the other delegates are reliable?

from **The Federalist Papers**
by Alexander Hamilton and James Madison

The Federalist is a name given to a collection of essays that were written by Alexander Hamilton, James Madison, and John Jay in 1787. They wrote the essays to persuade people in the separate states to accept the new federal Constitution. The first passage that follows is by Alexander Hamilton, and it introduces the series. The second passage is by James Madison. In it, Madison discusses the many advantages of the new system of government.

Number 1 (Hamilton)

After an unequivocal experience of the inefficiency of the subsisting federal government, you are called upon to deliberate on a new Constitution for the United States of America. The subject speaks its own importance; comprehending in its consequences nothing less than the existence of the UNION, the safety and welfare of the parts of which it is composed, the fate of an empire in many respects the most interesting in the world. It has been frequently remarked that it seems to have been reserved to the people of this country, by their conduct and example, to decide the important question, whether societies of men are really capable or not of establishing good government from reflection and choice, or whether they are forever destined to depend for their political constitutions on accident and force. If there be any truth in the remark, the crisis at which we are arrived may with propriety be regarded as the era in which that decision is to be made; and a wrong election of the part we shall act may, in this view, deserve to be considered as the general misfortune of mankind.

This idea will add the inducements of philanthropy to those of patriotism, to heighten the solicitude which all considerate and good men must feel for the event. Happy will it be if our choice should be directed by a judicious estimate of our true interests, unperplexed and unbiased by considerations not connected with the public good. But this is a thing more ardently to be wished than seriously to be expected. The plan offered to our deliberations affects too many particular interests, innovates upon too many local institutions, not to involve in its discussion a variety of objects foreign to its merits, and of views, passions, and prejudices little favorable to the discovery of truth.

Among the most formidable of the obstacles which the new Constitution will have to encounter may readily be distinguished the obvious interest of a certain class of men in every state to resist all changes which may hazard a diminution of the power, emolument, and consequence of the offices they hold under the state establishments; and the perverted ambitions of another class of men, who will either hope to aggrandize themselves by the confusions of their country, or will flatter themselves with fairer prospects of elevation from the subdivision of the empire into several partial confederacies than from its union under one government.

Number 10 (Madison)

Among the numerous advantages promised by a well constructed union, none deserves to be more accurately developed than its tendency to break and control the violence of faction. . . . The instability, injustice, and confusion introduced into the

unequivocal   very clear in meaning; plain
inefficiency   a wasting of time, energy or material
inducements   the act of persuading or leading a person into doing something
philanthropy   a strong wish to help people, shown by giving large sums of money to causes that help other people
solicitude   care; worry; concern

formidable   causing fear or dread
diminution   a lessening in size or amount
emolument   payment for an office or a job
aggrandize   to make more powerful
faction   a group of people inside a government working together against other such groups for its own ideas or goals

public councils have, in truth, been the mortal diseases under which popular governments have everywhere perished. . . . The valuable improvements made by the American Constitution on the popular models, both ancient and modern, cannot certainly be too much admired; but it would be an unwarranted partiality to contend that they have as effectually obviated the danger on this side, as was wished and expected. Complaints are everywhere heard from our most considerate and virtuous citizens, equally the friends of public and private faith and of public and personal liberty, that our governments are too unstable, that the public good is disregarded in the conflicts of rival parties, and that measures are too often decided, not according to the rules of justice and the rights of the minor party, but by the superior force of an interested and overbearing majority. . . . It will be found, indeed, on a candid review of our situation, that some of the distresses under which we labor have been erroneously charged on the operation of our governments; but it will be found, at the same time, that other causes will not alone account for many of our heaviest misfortunes. . . . These must be chiefly, if not wholly, effects of the unsteadiness and injustice with which a factious spirit has tainted our public administrations.

candid   frank, honest, and fair

Think It Over

1. People often try to win support by attacking their opponents. Give one example of how Hamilton attacks the Antifederalists.

2. How does Madison's view of government compare with Hamilton's?

from **The Magna Carta**

On June 15, 1215, King John of England made peace with rebellious barons by agreeing to sign the Magna Carta. The Magna Carta contained the barons' demands for reforms that increased the barons' rights and limited the king's power. The document established the principle that the king has to obey the law of the land. The Magna Carta became the basis for democratic government in England. Later, in 1787, American statesmen used the democratic principles found in the Magna Carta in writing the Constitution of the United States.

John, by the grace of God, king of England, lord of Ireland, duke of Normandy and Aquitaine, count of Anjou to the archbishops, bishops, abbots, earls, barons, justiciars, foresters, sheriffs, reeves, servants, and all his bailiffs and his faithful people greeting. . . .

1. In the first place we have granted to God and by this our present charter confirmed for us and our heirs forever that the English church shall be free, and shall hold its rights entire, and her liberties inviolate. . . . We have granted moreover to all free men of our kingdom for us and our heirs forever all the liberties written below, to be held by them and their heirs from us and our heirs forever. . . .

8. No widow shall be compelled to marry, so long as she prefers to live without a husband; provided always that she gives security not to marry without our consent, if she holds of us,* or without the consent of the lord of whom she holds, if she holds of another.

9. Neither we nor our bailiffs shall seize any land or rent for any debt, so long as the chattels of the debtor are sufficient to repay the debt. . . .

14. And for holding a common council of the kingdom concerning the assessment of an aid [tax] . . . we shall cause to be summoned the archbishops, bishops, abbots, earls, and greater barons . . . we shall cause to be summoned by our sheriffs and bailiffs, all others who hold of us in chief, for a fixed date . . . and at a fixed place; and in all letters of such summons we will specify the reason of the summons. And when the summons has thus been made, the business shall proceed on the day appointed, according to the counsel of such as are present, although not all who were summoned have come. . . .

28. No constable or other bailiff of ours shall take corn or other provisions from any one without immediately tendering money therefor, unless he can have postponement thereof by permission of the seller. . . .

30. No sheriff or bailiff of ours, or other person, shall take the horses or carts of any freeman for transport duty, against the will of the said freeman.

31. Neither we nor our bailiffs shall take, for our castles or for any other work of ours, wood which is not ours, against the will of the owner of that wood. . . .

---

* To "hold of" meant to live on land granted by the king or by another lord.

inviolate   not broken; kept sacred
compelled   forced
bailiffs   sheriff's assistants
chattels   pieces of property that can be moved, such as livestock
assessment   the act of estimating how much a property is worth in order to figure the tax on it

abbots   men who are head of abbeys of monks; church leaders
counsel   advice or opinion
constable   police officer
provisions   supplies
tendering   presenting; offering
postponement   a delay

38. No bailiff for the future shall, upon his own unsupported complaint, put anyone to his "law," without credible witness brought for this purpose.

39. No free man shall be taken, or imprisoned, or dispossessed, or outlawed, or banished, or in any way destroyed, except by the legal judgment of his peers or by the law of the land.

40. To no one will we sell, to no one will we deny, or delay, right or justice.

credible   believable
dispossessed   forced by law to give up property

peers   people of the same rank or age; equals

Think It Over

1. The Magna Carta was originally written in an earlier form of English and has been translated into modern English. Why is it important to know whether a document has been translated?

A Description of George Washington
by Thomas Jefferson

Thomas Jefferson, author of the Declaration of Independence, knew all the chief leaders of the Revolution and the new republic. He himself served as third President of the United States. He also wrote on many subjects ranging from philosophy, religion, and science to education and farming. As he grew older, he was often asked about leaders of the Revolutionary era. This excerpt is from a letter Jefferson wrote to Dr. Walter Jones, who had asked about George Washington.

I think I knew General Washington intimately and thoroughly; and were I called on to delineate his character, it should be in terms like these.

His mind was great and powerful, without being of the very first order; his penetration [keenness of mind] strong, though not so acute as that of a Newton, Bacon, or Locke; and as far as he saw, no judgment was ever sounder. It was slow in operation, being little aided by invention or imagination, but sure in conclusion. Hence the common remark of his officers, of the advantage he derived [gained] from councils of war, where hearing all suggestions, he selected whatever was best; and certainly no General ever planned his battles more judiciously. But if deranged [upset] during the course of the action, if any member of his plan was dislocated by sudden circumstances, he was slow in readjustment. The consequence was, that he often failed in the field, and rarely against an enemy in station, as in Boston and York.

He was incapable of fear, meeting personal dangers with the calmest unconcern. Perhaps the strongest feature in his character was prudence, never acting until every circumstance, every consideration, was maturely weighed; refraining if he saw a doubt, but, when once decided, going through with his purpose, whatever obstacles opposed. . . .

His heart was not warm in its affections; but he exactly calculated every man's value, and gave him a solid esteem proportioned to it. His person, you know, was fine, his stature exactly what one would wish, his deportment [bearing] easy, erect and noble; the best horseman of his age, and the most graceful figure that could be seen on horseback. Although in the circle of his friends, where he might be unreserved with safety, he took a free share in conversation, his colloquial talents were not above mediocrity, possessing neither copiousness of ideas, nor fluency of words. In public, when called on for a sudden opinion, he was unready, short and embarrassed. Yet he wrote readily, rather diffusely [wordily], in an easy and correct style. . . .

On the whole, his character was, in its mass, perfect, in nothing bad, in a few points indifferent; and it may truly be said, that never did nature and fortune combine more perfectly to make a man great, and to place him in the same constellation with whatever worthies have merited from man an everlasting remembrance.

delineate   describe
acute   sharp
judiciously   wisely
prudence   the act of being careful or cautious and not taking chances
colloquial   conversational
mediocrity   the quality of being of ordinary ability

copiousness   greatness in number
fluency   the quality of speaking easily and clearly
indifferent   neither good nor bad
constellation   a group of stars; here: an elevated position
worthies   very important people

Think It Over

1. Would you consider Thomas Jefferson to be a reliable source of information about George Washington? Why or why not?

from **Washington's Farewell Address**
by George Washington

In 1796, after serving two terms as President, George Washington wrote his famous Farewell Address. In it, he announced that he would not seek a third term. As he retired from public service, the outgoing President gave his views on the best policies for the young republic to follow. As the nation's first President, he knew firsthand the great issues of the day. He was especially concerned about the rise of political parties and the danger of the nation becoming involved in European wars. Washington's advice about foreign policy influenced future Presidents for more than a century. The following excerpt is from Washington's Farewell Address.

FRIENDS AND FELLOW-CITIZENS:

The period for a new election of a citizen, to administer the executive government of the United States, being not far distant . . . , it appears to me proper, . . . that I should now apprise you of the resolution I have formed to decline being considered among the number of those out of whom a choice is to be made. . . .

I have already intimated [suggested] to you the danger of parties in the State, with particular reference to the founding of them on geographical discriminations [bases]. Let me now take a more comprehensive view, and warn you in the most solemn manner against the baneful effects of the spirit of party, generally. . . .

It serves always to distract the public councils and enfeeble the public administration. It agitates the community with ill-founded jealousies and false alarms, kindles the animosity of one part against another, foments occasionally riot and insurrection. It opens the door to foreign influence and corruption, which find a facilitated access to the government itself through the channels of party passions. Thus the policy and the will of one country, are subjected to the policy and will of another. . . .

Observe good faith and justice toward all nations. Cultivate peace and harmony with all. Religion and morality enjoin this conduct and can it be that good policy does not equally enjoin it? It will be worthy of a free, enlightened, and at no distant period, a great nation, to give to mankind the magnanimous and too novel example of a people always guided by an exalted justice and benevolence. . . .

The great rule of conduct for us in regard to foreign nations is, in extending our commercial relations to have with them as little political connection as possible. So far as we have already formed engagements let them be fulfilled, with perfect good faith. Here let us stop.

Europe has a set of primary interests which to us have none, or a very remote relation. Hence she must be engaged in frequent controversies, the causes of which are essentially foreign to our concerns. . . .

Our detached and distant situation invites and enables us to pursue a different course. If we remain one people, under an efficient government, the period is not far off when we may defy material injury from external [outside] annoyance; when we may take such an attitude as will cause the neutrality we may at any time resolve upon to be scrupulously [carefully] respected; when belligerent [warring] nations, under the impossibility of making acquisitions upon us, will not lightly

apprise to let know; inform
baneful causing worry
enfeeble to make weak
agitate to stir up or shake up
animosity a feeling of strong dislike or hate
foment to excite or stir up trouble

facilitated access easy entry
enjoin to order or command
magnanimous generous in forgiving; not mean or petty
benevolence a tendency to do good; kindliness; generosity

hazard [risk] the giving us provocation; when we may choose peace or war, as our interest, guided by justice, shall counsel. . . .

It is our true policy to steer clear of permanent alliances with any portion of the foreign world, so far, I mean as we are now at liberty to do it; for let me not be understood as capable of patronizing [supporting] infidelity [unfaithfulness] to existing engagements. I hold the maxim no less applicable to public than to private affairs that honesty is always the best policy. I repeat, therefore, let those engagements be observed in their genuine sense. But in my opinion it is unnecessary and would be unwise to extend them.

Taking care always to keep ourselves by suitable establishments on a respectable defensive posture, we may safely trust to temporary alliances for extraordinary emergencies.

provocation   something that excites people to some action or feeling

maxim   a short saying that has become a rule of conduct

Think It Over

1. How does Washington think the United States should behave toward other nations? Why does he give that advice?

2. Washington himself belonged to no political party. Do you think that fact increases or decreases the effectiveness of what he has to say about parties?

Traveling With Lewis and Clark
from *Bird Woman* by Sacajawea

A Shoshone woman named Sacajawea, her husband, and her baby son Pomp accompanied Lewis and Clark on their expedition across the Louisiana Territory. As a child Sacajawea had been kidnapped from her Mandan village by the Minnetarees, a rival Native American group. She was adopted by a Minnetaree family and lived in their village. Sacajawea met Lewis and Clark when they camped at the Minnetaree village. Years later, Sacajawea told her life story to James Willard Schultz. This passage is from Sacajawea's autobiography, *Bird Woman*. In this passage, Sacajawea refers to Lewis and Clark as Long Knife and Red Hair.

Upon my man's return to the fort the boats were all loaded. We had two large ones and six small ones, and we abandoned the fort and headed up river. At the same time that we started, Long Knife and Red Hair sent their very large boat down the river in charge of some of their men. It was loaded with many skins, bones, and other things, presents for the great chief of the whites. Counting in my son, we were thirty-three people in our eight boats. I was given a place in one of the two large ones.

As we went on and on up the river, sometimes making a long distance between the rising and the setting of the sun, I was, at times, I believe, happier than I had ever been in my life, for each day's travel brought me so much nearer my people whom I so much longed to see. Then at other times, whenever I thought of what was before us, I would become very unhappy. I would say to myself that we could not possibly survive the dangers we should be sure to encounter along the way. I may as well say it: my good, kind white chiefs were not cautious; they were too brave, too sure of themselves. From the very start they and their men would foolishly risk their lives by attacking all the mankilling bears that came in sight of us. At night they would build great fires and would be sure to attract to us any wandering war party that might be in the country. After we passed the mouth of the Yellowstone and entered the country of the Blackfeet, I begged my chiefs to be more cautious. I asked them to stop always a short time before dark and build

little cooking-fires, and then, after our meal, to put out the fires, and then go on until dark and make camp in the darkness. But they only laughed at me and answered: "We have good guns and know how to use them."

I often said to myself: "Strange are these white men! Strange their ways! They have a certain thing to do, to make a trail to the west to the Everywhere-Salt-Water. Why, then, are we not on horseback and traveling fast and far each day? Here we are in boats, heavily loaded with all kinds of useless things, and when the wind is bad or the water swift, we make but little distance between sun and sun! We could have all got all the horses that we needed from the Earth House tribes, and had we done that, we should long since have arrived at the mountains. Yes, right now I should probably be talking with my own people!"

And those medicine packages of theirs, packages big and little piled all around me in the boat in which I rode, how my chiefs valued them! One day a sudden hard wind struck our sail and the boat began to tip and fill with water. More and more it filled, and the men in it and those on the shore went almost crazy with fear. But I was not afraid. Why should I be when I knew that I could cast off my robe and swim ashore with my little son? More and more water poured into the boat and the medicine packages began to float out of it. I seized them one by one as they were going, and kept seizing them and holding them, and when, at last, we reached the shore, my good white chiefs acted as

abandoned   gave up completely

though I had done a wonderful thing in saving their packages; it seemed as though they could not thank me enough for what I had done. Thinking about it, after it was all over, and when the things had been spread out to dry, I said to myself: "Although I cannot understand them, these little instruments of shining steel and these writings on thin white paper must be powerful medicine. Hereafter, whenever we run into danger, I shall, after my son, have my first thought for their safety, and so please my kind white chiefs."

After leaving the mouth of Little River, or, as my white chiefs named it, Milk River, we went up through a part of the Big River Valley that I had not seen. . . . When we arrived at the mouth of the stream my white chiefs named the Musselshell, some of the men went up it during the afternoon, and, returning, told of a stream coming into it from the plain on the right. My chiefs then told me that it should have my name, as they called it, Sah-ka-já-we-ah.

I asked my man to tell them that I wished they would give it my right name, Bo-í-naiv, Grass Woman.

Think It Over

1. Sacajawea told her life story to writer James Willard Schultz, who published it in 1918. Identify two factors that might affect the reliability of the published account.

from *The Pioneers*
by James Fenimore Cooper

James Fenimore Cooper wrote action-filled adventure stories that were very popular. The central character in five of his novels is a wilderness hunter named Natty Bumppo, or Leather-stocking, who lives between the Indian and white worlds. Bumppo has learned the forest skills of the Indians. This selection is from *The Pioneers*. In this scene, Leather-stocking realizes that the wilderness is fast falling to settlers.

If the heavens were alive with pigeons, the whole village seemed equally in motion, with men, women, and children. Every species of fire-arms, from the French ducking-gun, with a barrel near six feet in length, to the common horseman's pistol, was to be seen in the hands of the men and boys; while bows and arrows, some made of the simple stick of a walnut sapling, and others in a rude [simple] imitation of the ancient cross-bows, were carried by many of the latter. . . .

Amongst the sportsmen was the tall, gaunt form of Leather-stocking, walking over the field, with his rifle hanging on his arm, his dogs at his heels; the latter now scenting the dead or wounded birds, that were beginning to tumble from the flocks, and then crouching under the legs of their master, as if they participated in his feelings, at this wasteful and unsportsmanlike execution.

The reports of the fire-arms became rapid, whole volleys rising from the plain, as flocks of more than ordinary numbers darted over the opening, shadowing the field, like a cloud; and then the light smoke of a single piece would issue from among the leafless bushes on the mountain, as death was hurled on the retreat of the affrighted birds, who were rising from a volley, in a vain effort to escape. Arrows, and missiles of every kind, were in the midst of the flocks; and so numerous were the birds, and so low did they take their flight, that even long poles, in the hands of those on the sides of the mountain, were used to strike them to the earth. . . .

So prodigious was the number of birds, that the scattering fire of the guns, with the hurling of missiles, and the cries of the boys, had no other effect than to break off small flocks from the immense masses that continued to dart along the valley, as if the whole of the feathered tribe were pouring through one pass. None pretended to collect the game, which lay scattered over the fields in such profusion, as to cover the very ground with the fluttering victims.

Leather-stocking was a silent, but uneasy spectator of all these proceedings [events], but was able to keep his sentiments to himself until he saw the introduction of the swivel [cannon] into the sports.

"This comes of settling a country!" he said—"here have I known the pigeons to fly for forty long years, and, till you made your clearings, there was nobody to skear [scare] or to hurt them. I loved to see them come into the woods, for they were company to a body; hurting nothing; being, as it was, as harmless as a garter-snake. But now it gives me sore thoughts when I hear the frighty things whizzing through the air, for I know it's only a motion to bring out all the brats in the village. Well! the Lord won't see the waste of his creaters for nothing, and right will be done to the pigeons, as well as others, by-and-by. . . ."

Among the sportsmen was Billy Kirby, who, armed with an old musket, was loading, and, without even looking into the air, was firing, and shouting as his victims fell even on his own person. He heard the speech of Natty, and took upon himself to reply—

species   kinds or sorts
sapling   a young tree
gaunt   so thin that bones show
vain   without success

prodigious   very great; enormous
profusion   a great or generous amount
uneasy   not comfortable
sentiments   feelings

"What! old Leather-stocking," he cried, "grumbling at the loss of a few pigeons! If you had to sow your wheat twice, and three times, as I have done, you wouldn't be so massy-fully [mercifully] feeling'd to'wards the divils.—Hurrah, boys! scatter the feathers. This is better than shooting at a turkey's head and neck, old fellow."

"It's better for you, maybe, Billy Kirby," replied the indignant old hunter, "and all them that don't know how to put a ball down a rifle-barrel, or how to bring it up ag'in with a true aim; but it's wicked to be shooting into flocks in this wastey manner; and none do it, who know how to knock over a single bird. If a body has a craving for pigeon's flesh, why! it's made the same as all other creater's, for man's eating, but not to kill twenty and eat one."

indignant   angry about something that seems unfair

Think It Over

1. Fiction writers often express their views through the mouths of their characters. Which character do you think expresses Cooper's view: Leather-stocking or Kirby? Give reasons for your answer.

2. How is Natty Bumppo's conflict with the settlers similar to that between environmentalists and developers today?

Working in the Lowell Mills
from *Loom and Spindle* by Harriot Hanson Robinson

In 1898, Harriet Hanson Robinson published a book, *Loom and Spindle,* which tells of her experiences working in the Lowell, Massachusetts, textile mills in the 1830's. In the following passage, Robinson describes life in Lowell, and tells about the first strike there.

In 1831 Lowell was little more than a factory village. Several corporations were started, and the cotton-mills belonging to them were building. Help was in great demand; and stories were told all over the country of the new factory town, and the high wages that were offered to all classes of workpeople—stories that reached the ears of mechanics' and farmers' sons, and gave new life to lonely and dependent women in distant towns and farmhouses. Into this Yankee El Dorado,* these needy people began to pour by the various modes of travel known to those slow old days. The stagecoach and the canal boat came everyday, always filled with new recruits for this army of useful people. The mechanic and machinist came, each with his home-made chest of tools, and often-times his wife and little ones. The widow came with her little flock and her scanty housekeeping goods to open a boarding-house or variety store, and so provided a home for her fatherless children. Many farmers' daughters came to earn money to complete their wedding outfit, or buy the bride's share of housekeeping articles. . . .

One of the first strikes of cotton factory operatives that ever took place in this country was that in Lowell, in October 1836. When it was announced that the wages were to be cut down, great indignation was felt, and it was decided to strike, *en masse.* This was done. The mills were shut down, and the girls went in procession from their several corporations to the "grove" on Chapel Hill, and listened to "incendiary" speeches from early labor reformers.

One of the girls stood on a pump, and gave vent to the feelings of her companions in a neat speech, declaring that it was their duty to resist all attempts at cutting down the wages. This was the first time a woman had spoken in public in Lowell, and the event caused surprise and consternation among her audience.

Cutting down the wages was not their only grievance, nor the only cause of the strike. Hitherto the corporations had paid twenty-five cents a week towards the board of each operative, and now it was their purpose to have the girls pay the sum; and this, in addition to the cut in wages, would make a difference of at least one dollar a week. . . .

My own recollection of this first strike (or "turn out" as it was called) is very vivid. I worked in a lower room, where I had heard the proposed strike fully, if not vehemently, discussed; I had been an ardent listener to what was said against this attempt at "oppression" on the part of the corporation, and naturally I took sides with the strikers. When the day came on which the girls were to turn out, those in the upper rooms started first, and so many of them left that our mill was at once shut down. Then, when the girls in my room stood irresolute, uncertain what to do, asking each other, "Would you?" or "Shall we turn out?" and not one of them having the courage to lead off, I, who began to think they would not go out, after

---

*El Dorado refers to a place rich in opportunity to become wealthy.

modes   methods
incendiary   stirring up trouble
consternation   great fear or shock that makes one feel helpless or confused

ardent   full of eagerness; enthusiastic
irresolute   not able to decide or make up one's mind

all their talk, became impatient, and started on ahead, saying, with childish bravado, "I don't care what you do, I am going to turn out, whether any one else does or not"; and I marched out, and was followed by the others. . . .

It is hardly necessary to say that so far as results were concerned this strike did no good. The dissatisfaction of the operatives subsided, or burned itself out, and though the authorities did not accede to their demands, the majority returned to their work, and the corporation went on cutting down the wages.

accede   to give one's consent

Think It Over

1. How did the author view the cotton-mill workers?

2. How much of what Robinson reports did she witness herself? How much did she learn from other sources?

Name _____   Date _____

from **The Monroe Doctrine**
by James Madison

In his State of the Union message to Congress in December 1823, James Monroe issued a warning to European powers not to try to extend their influence in the Western Hemisphere. His warning, which has come to be known as the Monroe Doctrine, had immediate implications. At the time, Russia threatened to encroach in the far Northwest, Great Britain showed some interest in acquiring Cuba, and it was thought that the Quadruple Alliance* wanted to help Spain recover its lost American colonies. The following passage includes relevant excerpts from the Monroe Doctrine.

Annual Message
December 2, 1823

Fellow-citizens of the Senate and House of Representatives:

. . . At the proposal of the Russian Imperial Government, made through the minister of the Emperor residing here, a full power and instructions have been transmitted to the ministers of the United States at St. Petersburg to arrange by amicable negotiations the respective rights and interests of the two nations on the northwest coast of this continent. A similar proposal had been made by His Imperial Majesty to the government of Great Britain, which had likewise been acceded to. The government of the United States has been desirous, by this friendly proceeding, of manifesting the great value which they have invariably attached to the friendship of the Emperor and their solicitude to cultivate the best understanding with his government. In the discussions to which this interest has given rise and in the arrangements by which they may terminate, the occasion has been judged proper for asserting, as a principle in which the rights and interests of the United States are involved, that the American continents, by the free and independent condition which they have assumed

and maintain, are henceforth not considered as subject for future colonization by any European powers. . . .

The citizens of the United States cherish sentiments the most friendly in favor of the liberty and happiness of their fellow men on that side of the Atlantic. In the wars of the European powers in matters relating to themselves we have never taken any part, nor does it comport with our policy so to do. It is only when our rights are invaded or seriously menaced that we resent injuries or make preparations for our defense. With the movements in this hemisphere we are of necessity more immediately connected, and by causes which must be obvious to all enlightened and impartial observers. The political system of the allied powers is essentially different in this respect from that of America. This difference proceeds from that which exists in their respective governments; and to the defense of our own, which has been achieved by the loss of so much blood and treasure, and matured by the wisdom of their most enlightened citizens, and under which we have enjoyed unexampled felicity, this whole nation is devoted. We owe it, therefore, to candor and to the amicable relations existing between the United States and those powers to declare that we should consider any attempt on their part to extend their system to any portion of this hemisphere as dangerous to our peace and safety. With the existing colonies or dependencies of

---

* The Quadruple Alliance was a group of European nations that worked together to achieve their goals. It included Britain, Austria, Prussia, and—later—France.

amicable friendly
acceded agreed
solicitude care, worry or concern
comport to agree or fit in

felicity happiness
candor honesty and openness in saying what one thinks; frankness

any European power we shall not interfere. But with the governments who have declared their independence and maintained it, and whose independence we have, on great consideration and on just principles, acknowledged, we could not view any interposition for the purpose of oppressing them or controlling in any other manner their destiny, by any European power in any other light than as the manifestation of an unfriendly disposition toward the United States. . . .

Our policy in regard to Europe, which was adopted at an early stage of the wars which have so long agitated that quarter of the globe, nevertheless remains the same, which is, not to interfere in the internal concerns of any of its powers; to consider the government *de facto* as the legitimate government for us; to cultivate friendly relations by a frank, firm, and manly policy, meeting

de facto   actually; in fact

in all instances the just claims of every power, submitting to injuries from none. But in regard to those continents circumstances are eminently and conspicuously different. It is impossible that the allied powers should extend their political system to any portion of either continent without endangering our peace and happiness; nor can anyone believe that our southern brethren, if left to themselves, would adopt it of their own accord. It is equally impossible, therefore, that we should behold such interposition in any form with indifference. If we look to the comparative strength and resources of Spain and those new governments, and their distances from each other, it must be obvious that she can never subdue them. It is still the true policy of the United States to leave the parties to themselves, in the hope that other powers will pursue the same course.

eminently   remarkably; outstandingly

Think It Over

1. Monroe addressed this speech to "Fellow citizens of the Senate and House of Representatives." What other audience did he intend his message to reach?

Speech Against Nullification
by Daniel Webster

In 1830, Senator Robert Y. Hayne of South Carolina, representing the southern states, spoke in the Senate in support of states' rights and nullification. Senator Daniel Webster of Massachusetts then replied to Hayne. His dramatic speech, given over two days, became famous throughout the nation. The following excerpt is from Webster's reply to Hayne.

If anything be found in the national Constitution . . . which ought not be in it, the people know how to get rid of it. If any construction is established unacceptable to them, so as to become practically a part of the Constitution, they will amend it, at their own sovereign pleasure. But while the people choose to maintain it as it is, while they are satisfied with it, and refuse to change it, who has given, or who can give, to the state legislatures a right to alter it, either by interference, construction, or otherwise? Gentlemen do not seem to recollect that the people have any power to do anything for themselves. They imagine there is no safety for them, any longer than they are under the close guardianship of the state legislatures. . . .

The people of the United States have at no time, in no way, directly or indirectly, authorized any state legislature to construe or interpret *their* high instrument of government; much less to interfere, by their own power, to arrest its course and operation.

If, sir, the people in these respects had done otherwise than they have done, their Constitution could neither have been preserved, nor would it have been worthy preserving. And if its plain provisions shall now be disregarded, and these new doctrines interpolated in it, it will become as feeble and helpless a being as its enemies, whether early or more recent, could possibly desire. It will exist in every state but as a poor dependent on state permission. . . .

But, sir, although there are fears, there are hopes also. The people have preserved this, their own chosen Constitution, for forty years, and have seen their happiness, prosperity, and renown grow with its growth, and strengthen with its strength. They are now, generally, strongly, attached to it. Overthrown by direct assault, it cannot be; evaded, undermined, *nullified*, it will not be, if we, and those who shall succeed us here, as agents and representatives of the people, shall conscientiously and vigilantly discharge the two great branches of our public trust, faithfully to preserve, and wisely to administer it. . . .

While the Union lasts, we have high, exciting, gratifying prospects spread out before us, for us and our children. . . . Liberty *and* Union, now and forever, one and inseparable!

sovereign   not controlled by others
construe   to explain the meaning of
interpolated   inserted

conscientiously   with great care
vigilantly   watchfully

Think It Over

1. In their speeches, politicians often use emotional appeals to rally support for a particular cause. How do Webster's final words appeal to his listeners' emotions? How do you think he used his voice to increase the effect of his words?

from *The Cherokee Removal*
by Evan Jones

The Indian Removal Act forced the Cherokee, the Creek, the Chickasaw, and the Choctaw to resettle west of the Mississippi. When it came time for the Cherokees to leave their homes in 1838, many resisted. Evan Jones, a Baptist missionary, worked among the Cherokee in North Carolina and joined them on their westward march. The following excerpt is from a series of letters written by Jones.

Camp Hetzel, Near Cleveland, June 16

The Cherokees are nearly all prisoners. They have been dragged from their houses, and encamped at the forts and military posts, all over the nation. In Georgia, especially, multitudes were allowed no time to take anything with them, except the clothes they had on. Well-furnished houses were a prey to plunderers, who, like hungry wolves, follow in the train of the captors. These wretches rifle the houses, and strip the helpless, unoffending owners of all they have on earth. . . . The property of many has been taken, and sold before their eyes for almost nothing—the sellers and buyers, in many cases, being combined to cheat the poor Indians. . . . The poor captive, in a state of distressing agitation, his weeping wife almost frantic with terror, surrounded by a group of crying, terrified children, without a friend to speak a consoling word, is in a poor condition to make a good disposition of his property and is in most cases stripped of the whole, at one blow. Many of the Cherokees, who, a few days ago, were in comfortable circumstances, are now victims of abject poverty. Some, who have been allowed to return home, under passport, to inquire after their property, have found their cattle, horses, swine, farming tools, and house furniture all gone. And this is not a description of extreme cases. It is altogether a faint representation of the work which has been perpetrated on the unoffending, unarmed, and unresisting Cherokees. . . .

It is due to justice to say, that, at this station (and I learn the same is true of some others), the officer in command treats his prisoners with great respect and indulgence. But fault rests somewhere. They are prisoners, without a crime to justify the fact. . . .

July 10 and July 11

The work of war in time of peace, is commenced in the Georgia part of the Cherokee nation, and is carried on, in most cases, in the most unfeeling and brutal manner; no regard being paid to the orders of the commanding General, in regard to humane treatment of the Indians. I have heard of only one officer in Georgia (I hope there are more), who manifests anything like humanity, in his treatment of this persecuted people. . . .

The work of capturing being completed, and about 3,000 sent off, the General had agreed to suspend the further transportation of the captives till the first of September. This arrangement, though but a small favor, diffused universal joy through the camps of the prisoners. . . .

On our way, we met a detachment of 1,300 prisoners. As I took some of them by

plunderers   people who rob or take things by force
wretches   unhappy or miserable people
agitation   excitement or emotional disturbance
consoling   making less sad or troubled; comforting

disposition   the act of getting rid of
perpetrated   committed; carried out
manifests   reveals; shows plainly

hand, the tears gushed from their eyes. Their hearts, however, were cheered to see us, and to hear a word of consolation. Many members of the church were among them. At Fort Butler, we found a company of 300, just arrived from the mountains, on their way to the general depot, at the agency. Several of our members were among these also.

Think It Over

1. Did Evan Jones directly witness everything he describes in his letters? Explain.

2. Based on the excerpt, how did Evan Jones view the United States Army's treatment of the Cherokees?

from *Death Comes for the Archbishop*
by Willa Cather

Many of the novels of Willa Cather focus on pioneer life on the Great Plains. In *Death Comes for the Archbishop,* however, her setting is the American Southwest during the 1850's. The book's main character, Bishop Jean Latour, journeys with his Native American guide, Jacinto, through Arizona and New Mexico. In the following selection, Latour and Jacinto camp for the night during a journey to a distant mission.

Jacinto got firewood and good water from the Lagunas, and they made their camp in a pleasant spot on the rocks north of the village. As the sun dropped low, the light brought the white church and the yellow adobe houses up into relief from the flat ledges. Behind their camp, not far away, lay a group of great mesas. The Bishop asked Jacinto if he knew the name of the one nearest them.

"No, I do not know any name," he shook his head. "I know Indian name," he added, as if, for once, he were thinking aloud.

"And what is the Indian name?"

"The Laguna Indians call Snow-Bird mountain." He spoke somewhat unwillingly.

"That is very nice," said the Bishop musingly. "Yes, that is a pretty name. . . ."

The Bishop sat drinking his coffee slowly out of the tin cup, keeping the pot near the embers. The sun had set now, the yellow rocks were turning grey, down in the pueblo the light of the cook fires made red patches of the glassless windows, and the smell of [pine] smoke came softly through the still air.

The whole western sky was the color of golden ashes, with here and there a flush of red on the lip of a little cloud. High above the horizon the evening-star flickered like a lamp just lit, and close beside it was another star of constant light, much smaller. . . .

The two companions sat, each thinking his own thoughts as night closed in about them; a blue night set with stars, the bulk of the solitary mesas cutting into the firmament. The Bishop seldom questioned Jacinto about his thoughts or beliefs. He didn't think it polite, and he believed it to be useless. There

was no way he could transfer his own memories of European civilization into the Indian mind, and he was quite willing to believe that behind Jacinto there was a long tradition, a store of experience, which no language could translate to him. A chill came with the darkness. Father Latour put on his old fur-lined cloak, and Jacinto, loosening the blanket tied about his loins, drew it up over his head and shoulders.

"Many stars," he said presently. "What do you think about the stars, Padre?"

"The wise men tell us they are worlds like ours, Jacinto. . . ."

"I think not," [Jacinto] said in the tone of one who has considered a proposition fairly and rejected it. "I think they are leaders—great spirits."

"Perhaps they are," said the Bishop with a sigh. "Whatever they are, they are great. Let us say *Our Father,* and go to sleep, my boy."

Kneeling on either side of the embers they repeated the prayer together and then rolled up in their blankets. The Bishop went to sleep thinking with satisfaction that he was beginning to have some sort of human companionship with his Indian boy. One called the young Indians "boys," perhaps because there was something youthful and elastic in their bodies. Certainly about their behavior there was nothing boyish in the American sense, nor even in the European sense. Jacinto was never, by any chance, [naive]; he was never taken by surprise. One felt that his training, whatever it had been, had prepared him to meet any situation which might confront him. He was as much at home in the Bishop's study as in his own

firmament   the sky

proposition   proposal, plan; here: concept or idea

pueblo—and he was never too much at home anywhere. Father Latour felt he had gone a good way toward gaining his guide's friendship, though he did not know how.

The truth was, Jacinto liked the Bishop's way of meeting people; thought he had the right tone with Padre Gallegos, the right tone with Padre Jesus, and that he had good manners with the Indians. In his experience, white people, when they addressed Indians, always put on a false face. There were many kinds of false faces; Father Vaillant's, for example, was kindly but too vehement. The Bishop put on none at all. He stood straight and turned to the Governor of Laguna, and his face underwent no change. Jacinto thought this remarkable.

vehement   full of deep, strong feeling; intense

Think It Over

1. Compare the bishop's and Jacinto's beliefs concerning the stars. What did each man think of the other's belief?

2. Willa Cather wrote *Death Comes for the Archbishop* in the 1920's— more than 70 years after the novel takes place. What kinds of historical sources could she have used to help her write her novel?

Eyewitness Account
★★★★★★
GEOGRAPHY

Trapped in the Sierra Nevada
from the diary of H. H. Bancroft

In 1846, a group of settlers started over the Sierra Nevada on their way to California. They were caught by an early winter snowstorm in what is now called Donner Pass. Of the 79 people in the party, only 45 survived. The following is an excerpt from the diary of H. H. Bancroft about the rescue of the trapped Donner party.

Foster had told us that we should find the emigrants at or near Truckee Lake, (since called Donner Lake) and in the direction of this we journeyed. Of course we had no guide, and most of our journey was through a dense pine forest, but the lofty peak which overlooks the lake was in sight at intervals, and this and the judgment of our two leaders were our sole means of direction. . . . When we started from the fort, Capt. Sutter assured us that we should be followed by other parties as soon as the necessary preparations could be made. For the guidance of those who might follow us and as a signal to any of the emigrants who might be straggling about in the mountains as well as for our own direction on our return trip, we set fire to every dead pine on or near our trail. . . .

At sunset of the 16th day we crossed Truckee Lake on the ice and came to the spot where we had been told we should find the emigrants. We looked all around but no living thing except ourselves was in sight and we thought that all must have perished. We raised a loud hello and then we saw a woman emerge from a hole in the snow. As we approached her several others made their appearance in like manner coming out of the snow. They were gaunt with famine and I never can forget the horrible, ghastly sight they presented. The first woman spoke in a hollow voice very much agitated and said, "Are you men from California or do you come from heaven?"

They had been without food except a few work oxen since the first fall of snow, about 3 weeks. They had gathered up the bones of the slaughtered cattle and boiled them to extract the grease and had roasted some of the hides which formed the roofs of their cabins. We gave them food very sparingly and retired for the night having some one of guard until morning to keep close watch on our provision to prevent the starving emigrants from eating them, which they would have done until they died of repletion.

When these emigrants had first been stopped by snow they had built small cabins using skins of the slaughtered oxen for roofs. Storms nearly continuous had caused the snow to fall to the depth of 18 feet so that the tops of their cabins were far beneath the surface. . . .

The morning after our arrival John P. Rhoads and Tucker started for another camp distant 8 miles east, where were the Donner family, to distribute what provisions could be spared and to bring along such of the party as had sufficient strength to walk. They returned bringing four girls and two boys of the Donner family and some others.

The next morning we started on our return trip accompanied by 21 emigrants mostly women and children. John Rhoads carried a child in his arms which died the second night. On the third day, an emigrant named John Denton, exhausted by starvation and totally snow-blind, gave out. He tried to keep up a hopeful and cheerful

emigrants   people who have left one country or region to settle in another
intervals   spaces and time between; gaps
famine   a great lack of food that causes people to starve throughout a wide region

provision   a supply of food
repletion   the condition of being full or filled up

appearance, but we knew he could not live much longer. We made a platform of saplings, built a fire on it, cut some boughs for him to sit upon and left him. This was imperatively necessary. The party who followed in our trail from California found his dead body a few days after we had left him, partially eaten by wolves.

imperatively   urgently

Think It Over

1. What information in this selection was Bancroft able to give as an eyewitness? What information did he have to get from members of the Donner party?

Three Views of Irish Immigration
from *Out of Ireland* by Kerby Miller and Paul Wagner

Under British rule, most farmland in Ireland was used to grow wheat and oats for sale outside of Ireland. Irish peasants depended on the potato for nourishment. Then, in 1845, disease destroyed the potato crop. To escape starvation, thousands of poor Irish families emigrated to the United States. In the first letter below, a young woman in Ireland describes the famine to her parents in Quebec, Canada. The second and third letters were written by new immigrants in New York to their villages back home.

Mary Rush:
Ardnaglass, Ireland
September 6, 1846

Dear Father and Mother,
    Pen cannot dictate the poverty of this country at present. The potato crop is quite done away all over Ireland. There is nothing expected here, only an immediate famine. If you knew what danger we and our fellow countrymen are suffering, if you were ever so much distressed, you would take us out of this poverty isle. We can only say, the scourge of God fell down on Ireland, in taking away the potatoes, they being the only support of the people. So, dear father and mother, if you don't endeavor to take us out of it, it will be the first news you will hear by some friend of me and my little family to be lost by hunger, and there are thousands dread they will share the same fate. So, I conclude with my blessings to you both. . . .
    For God's sake take us out of poverty, and don't let us die with the hunger.

Daniel Guiney:
Buffalo, New York
August 9, 1850

Dear Mother and Brothers,
    We mean to let you know our situation at present. We arrived here at five o'clock in the afternoon of yesterday, fourteen of us together, where we were received with the greatest kindness and respectability by Matthew Leary and Denis Danihy. When we came to the house we could not state to you how we were treated. We had potatoes, meat, butter, bread, and tea for dinner. . . .
    Dear friends, if you were to see old Denis Danihy, he never was in as good health and looks better than he ever did at home. . . . If you were to see Denis Reen when Daniel Danihy dressed him with clothes suitable for this country, you would think him to be a boss or steward, so that we have scarcely words to state to you how happy we felt at present. And as to the girls that used to be trotting on the bogs at home, to hear them talk English would be of great astonishment to you. Mary Keefe got two dresses, one from Mary Danihy and the other from Biddy Matt.

William Dever:
New York, New York
September 14, 1848

My dear Uncle and Brothers,
    It's inconceivable the thousands that land here every week from all the old countries flying from tyranny and oppression. Wealthy farmers with their whole families are coming here and purchasing farms, some the best land in the whole world. Germans, French, Hollanders are doing this on a large scale.
    But most of the Irish come out poor, unable to purchase farms. They work digging quarries, carrying brick and mortar in

scourge   something that causes great pain and suffering
endeavor   attempt; try
steward   a person hired to manage a large estate

inconceivable   unthinkable
quarries   places where stone is cut or blasted out of the earth

scorching sun up to the fourth stories of houses, in winter nothing to do, all their money spent. They are despised and kicked about. Many write home they are happy and wealthy, when they are of that class above mentioned. I heard friends of a young man in this city enquiring if John . . . was not a banker here, as he wrote home that he was so and persuaded all his relatives to come join him. But what was he, think you? He was sweeper of the office of the bank. They were astonished when told so. And thousands are just like him.

Think It Over

1. Explain how you think each of the following might have reacted if they had read Daniel Guiney's letter: (a) Mary Rush; (b) William Dever.

2. How does Dever's letter show why we cannot always take primary sources at face value?

Literature
★ ★ ★ ★ ★ ★

from *The Fires of Jubilee*
by Stephen B. Oates

In 1831, Nat Turner led a group of slaves on an uprising across Southampton County, Virginia. More than 50 white people were killed. Modern writer Stephen B. Oates wrote a dramatic account of this rebellion in *The Fires of Jubilee: Nat Turner's Fierce Rebellion.* The following excerpt describes the reaction of the white community after the rebellion.

In September, new alarms pummeled upper North Carolina. A man from Murfreesboro, having attended a slave trial in Virginia's Sussex County, reported back that the Southampton insurgents had expected armed slave resistance "from distant neighborhoods," including the large plantations on the Roanoke. Yes, the fellow cried, testimony in the Sussex trial "proved" that a concerted uprising was to have taken place in Virginia and upper North Carolina, where Negro preachers had been spreading disaffection, and that "dire and extensive would have been the slaughter but for a mistake in the day of commencement." The plan, the man said, called for the larger rebellion to begin on the last Sunday in August. But he contended that the Southampton rebels mistook August 21 as the target Sunday, all the while their North Carolina allies were waiting for August 28!

Though no such plan had existed, the report traumatized whites in the northeastern tier of counties, especially in neighborhoods with heavy slave concentrations. Couriers rode for Raleigh to beg for muskets and ammunition. Militia outfits mustered along the Roanoke, chased after imaginary insurgents and . . . imprisoned . . . still more innocent blacks. Phantom slave columns marched out of the Dismal Swamp, only to vanish when militia units rushed out to fight them.

In mid-September came the most shattering alarm of all: couriers reported that a full-scale rebellion had blazed up in southeastern North Carolina, in Duplin and Sampson counties. . . . Such communiqués were completely false, but frantic whites were now reacting to their own shadows. Militia commanders alerted their troops and sent off exaggerated reports to the governor, which gathered additional frills as express riders bore them to the capital. Meanwhile, mass hysteria gripped the town of Wilmington down near the Atlantic Ocean. . . .

But no slave army appeared. Out of blind vengeance, whites turned on the local Negro population and . . . forced five hapless blacks into confessing that, yes, they were to meet insurgents from Sampson County. . .

Raleigh too was in turmoil, as a succession of express riders burst into the city with doomsday reports: slave rebels had allegedly set much of eastern North Carolina afire. . . .

In all the excitement, a few people managed to keep their heads. On September 16, the Raleigh *Star* corrected its initial reports and denied the disturbing news now "circulating through the country." A few days later the Raleigh Register admitted that its own account of insurrections in North Carolina had been "highly exaggerated." The storm had passed now, the paper declared, so that it was possible to ascertain the truth. While slaves in the southeastern part of the state had undoubtedly "talked about insurrection," none in fact had transpired.

pummeled   beat or hit again and again
insurgents   rebels
disaffection   the state of being discontented
dire   very bad; dreadful; terrible

commencement   a beginning or start
couriers   messengers
communiqués   official messages
ascertain   to find out in such a way as to be sure

Think It Over

1. (a) On what information did the people in North Carolina base their belief that slaves were about to rebel? (b) What facts in the selection contradict those beliefs?

2. How can you tell that Stephen B. Oates did historical research before writing his book?

from *Narrative of the Life of Frederick Douglass*
by Frederick Douglass

Frederick Douglass escaped from slavery in 1838 and later became a leading abolitionist. From the money he earned writing and lecturing, Douglass was able to buy his freedom. In 1845, Douglass wrote *Narrative of the Life of Frederick Douglass*. In the following excerpt, Douglass explains why learning to read and write was so important to him.

My new mistress proved to be all she appeared when I first met her at the door—a woman of the kindest heart and finest feelings. She had never had a slave under her control previously to myself, and prior to her marriage she had been dependent upon her own industry for a living. She was by trade a weaver; and by constant application to her business, she had been in a good degree preserved from the blighting and dehumanizing effects of slavery. I was utterly astonished at her goodness. . . . She did not deem it impudent or unmannerly for a slave to look her in the face. The meanest slave was put fully at ease in her presence, and none left without feeling better for having seen her. Her face was made of heavenly smiles, and her voice of tranquil music.

But, alas! this kind heart had but a short time to remain such. The fatal poison of irresponsible power was already in her hands, and soon commenced its infernal work. That cheerful eye, under the influence of slavery, soon became red with rage. . . .

Very soon after I went to live with Mr. and Mrs. Auld, she very kindly commenced to teach me the A, B, C. After I had learned this, she assisted me in learning to spell words of three or four letters. Just at this point of my progress, Mr. Auld found out what was going on, and at once forbade Mrs. Auld to instruct me further, telling her, among other things, that it was unlawful, as well as unsafe, to teach a slave to read. To use his own words, further, he said, "If . . . you teach that nigger (speaking of myself) how to read, there would be no keeping him.

It would forever unfit him to be a slave. He would at once become unmanageable, and of no value to his master. As to himself, it could do him no good, but a great deal of harm. It would make him discontented and unhappy." These words sank deep into my heart, stirred up sentiments within that lay slumbering, and called into existence an entirely new train of thought. It was a new and special revelation, explaining dark and mysterious things, with which my youthful understanding had struggled, but struggled in vain. I now understood what had been to me a most perplexing difficulty—to wit, the white man's power to enslave the black man. It was a grand achievement, and I prized it highly. From that moment, I understood the pathway from slavery to freedom. It was just what I wanted, and I got it at a time when I the least expected it. Whilst I was saddened by the thought of losing the aid of my kind mistress, I was gladdened by the invaluable instruction which, by the merest accident, I had gained from my master. Though conscious of the difficulty of learning without a teacher, I set out with high hope, and a fixed purpose, at whatever cost of trouble, to learn how to read. The very decided manner with which he spoke, and strove to impress his wife with the evil consequences of giving me instruction, served to convince me that he was deeply sensible of the truths he was uttering. It gave me the best assurance that I might rely with the utmost confidence on the results which, he said, would flow from teaching me to read. What he most dreaded, that I most desired. What he most loved,

blighting   hurting, destroying
impudent   not showing respect
tranquil   calm
irresponsible   not showing a sense of duty; doing as one pleases

commenced   started; began
revelation   something revealed or making known, especially something surprising
perplexing   puzzling

that I most hated. That which to him was great evil, to be carefully shunned, was to me a great good, to be diligently sought; and the argument which he so warmly urged, against my learning to read, only served to inspire me with a desire and determination to learn. In learning to read, I owe almost as much to the bitter opposition of my master, as to the kindly aid of my mistress. I acknowledge the benefit of both.

Think It Over

1. According to the excerpt, how did Frederick Douglass view his master's opposition to educating slaves?

2. To gain support for what cause did Douglass write his autobiography? What made him an effective witness?

Declaration of Sentiments
adopted at the women's rights convention, Seneca Falls, New York, 1848

In 1848, Elizabeth Cady Stanton and Lucretia Mott led a women's rights convention in Seneca Falls, New York. The event marked the beginning of an organized women's rights movement in the United States. The women and men attending the convention adopted the following Declaration of Sentiments and a number of resolutions.

Declaration of Sentiments

When, in the course of human events, it becomes necessary for one portion of the family of man to assume among the people of the earth a position different from that which they have hitherto occupied, but one to which the laws of nature and of nature's God entitle them, a decent respect to the opinions of mankind requires that they should declare the causes that impel them to such a course.

We hold these truths to be self-evident that all men and women are created equal; that they are endowed by their Creator with certain inalienable rights; that among these are life, liberty, and the pursuit of happiness; that to secure these rights governments are instituted, deriving their just powers from the consent of the governed. Whenever any form of government becomes destructive of these ends, it is the right of those who suffer from it to refuse allegiance to it, and to insist upon the institution of a new government, laying its foundation on such principles, and organizing its powers in such form, as to them shall seem most likely to effect their safety and happiness. Prudence, indeed, will dictate that governments long established should not be changed for light and transient causes; and accordingly all experience hath shown that mankind are more disposed to suffer while evils are sufferable, than to right themselves by abolishing the forms to which they are accustomed. But when a long train of abuses and usurpations, pursuing invariably the same object, evinces a design to reduce them under absolute despotism, it is their duty to throw off such government, and to provide new guards for their future security. Such has been the patient sufferance of the women under this government, and such is now the necessity which constrains them to demand the equal station to which they are entitled.

The history of mankind is a history of repeated injuries and usurpations on the part of man toward woman, having in direct object the establishment of an absolute tyranny over her. To prove this, let facts be submitted to a candid world.

He has never permitted her to exercise her inalienable right to the elective franchise.

He has compelled her to submit to laws, in the formation of which she had no voice.

He has withheld from her rights which are given to the most ignorant and degraded men—both natives and foreigners.

Having deprived her of this first right of a citizen, the elective franchise, thereby leaving her without representation in the halls of legislation, he has oppressed her on all sides.

He has made her, if married, in the eye of the law, civilly dead.

He has taken from her all right in property, even to the wages she earns. . . .

impel   to push or move forward
endowed   provided with
inalienable   not able to be taken away or given away
allegiance   loyalty or devotion
prudence   the quality of careful or cautious actions and behavior
transient   staying only for a short time
usurpations   the act of taking and holding by force or without right

evinces   shows plainly, makes clear
despotism   a rule or government in which one person has complete control
constrains   forces
tyranny   cruel or unjust use of power
franchise   the right to vote

He has denied her the facilities for obtaining a thorough education, all colleges being closed against her. . . .

Resolutions

Resolved, That all laws which prevent woman from occupying such a station in society as her conscience shall dictate, or which place her in a position inferior to that of man, are contrary to the great precept of nature, and therefore of no force or authority.

Resolved, That woman is man's equal—was intended to be so by the Creator, and the highest good of the race demands that she should be recognized as such.

Resolved, That the women of this country ought to be enlightened in regard to the laws under which they live, that they may no longer publish their degradation by declaring themselves satisfied with their present position, nor their ignorance, by asserting that they have all the rights they want. . . .

Resolved, That the speedy success of our cause depends on the zealous and untiring efforts of both men and women. . . .

facilities   a building or room for some activity

zealous   very eager; enthusiastic

Think It Over

1. For what purpose was this document written?

2. Do you think it was intended to be read primarily by women, by men, or by both?

Literature
★★★★★

from *Caleb's Choice*
by G. Clifton Wisler

G. Clifton Wisler's novel *Caleb's Choice* is set in the late 1850's. Young Caleb Delaney goes to northern Texas to live with his grandmother and his cousins Edith and Micah. In Caleb's new home, people are divided over the Fugitive Slave Law. Caleb is not sure how he feels about the law. In the following excerpt, Caleb helps feed two captured fugitives.

You had to admit that they were good at their work. They captured the two runaways from Waco not a half mile from Spring Creek, and they located three others off a Smith County plantation.

"Already wired their owners," Ulysses boasted. "Mr. Francis Leighton will meet us in Dallas to take delivery of his two. Promised us a fifty-dollar bonus, too. We'll leave the other three with Sheriff Rutherford at McKinney. They're worth two hundred dollars altogether."

I thought about that. Papa needed five hundred dollars, and here the Fitches had earned almost that much capturing run- aways! The notion had a powerful pull to it. But when I followed Edith out to the well with some food for the prisoners, I realized that I would never have the heart to be a slave catcher. I recognized the two Waco slaves from the sketches on their posters, but I wasn't prepared for the other three. One was a sad-eyed girl no older than Edith, and the other two were slight-shouldered boys only a little taller than me. Not since departing Dallas had I seen people with such hollow eyes. Their feet were shackled, and their hands were bound with coarse rope that bit into the dark flesh of their wrists. The younger boy bled from the left side of his mouth. Edith gasped when she looked at the backs of the Waco runaways. The Fitches had used a whip on both.

"Fetch some water from the well," Edith told me.

"Already done," Polk Harrison announced, carrying a bucket over. "Spied them on the road."

Edith and Harrison exchanged an odd glance, and I sensed they wanted to say more. The runaways accepted cups of water gratefully, although with downcast eyes. The older ones managed to mumble a thank you when Edith promised to find some salve for their cuts. She placed slices of bread and chunks of ham in their fingers. They ate with considerable difficulty.

"We should notify the sheriff," Edith stormed. "Slaves or not, they don't deserve ill treatment."

"Its not illegal," Harrison argued. "There are slave catchers who do far worse. Fitches know better than to cut off a limb or ham- string a valuable hand. Takes away from the profit."

"They're getting a bonus," I pointed out. "Three hundred and fifty dollars in all."

"A man can always use money," Harrison admitted. "Me, I wouldn't take money earned from another man's bleeding."

"Even a slave?" I asked.

"Especially," Harrison said. "You accept a bounty for a killer, a man likely to hurt somebody else and capable of defending himself, that's one thing. But hunting down some poor wretch who only wants to be left alone?"

"That's pretty strong talk, mister," Ulysses said, walking over, rifle in hand. "You know, it wouldn't surprise me to learn somebody hereabouts hid those older ones. We looked mighty hard for 'em."

"That why you whipped them?" I asked, "To find out?"

"Oh, that was just a little message from Mr. Leighton," Ulysses explained. "Most likely

---

shackled bound with a metal loop put around the ankle
bounty a reward

wretch someone who is miserable or very unhappy; a person who is looked down on as low or worthless

they hid in a slave house at one of the big farms east of here. White men would know better than to help after that trouble on the Colorado River."

"What trouble?" I asked.

"Two years ago the authorities discovered a plot," Harrison told me. "Four hundred slaves were supposed to rise and kill their masters. . . ."

I shivered. Gazing into the eyes of those prisoners, though, I found it hard to imagine myself in much danger. Halfway starved and dressed in rags, they looked more like survivors off a Gulf shipwreck than bloodthirsty killers.

"Don't let 'em fool you, boy," Ulysses said to me in particular. "They hate us. . . ."

"Can't much blame them," Edith said, drawing me away from the well. "Lord know they've got reason enough."

"I suppose," I said, sighing. "I saw an auction in Dallas. I wouldn't want to be a slave. Desperate like that, they *could* be dangerous, though."

Think It Over

1. Why do you think that slave catchers were so well paid?

2. If you were writing a report about the attitudes of white Texans toward fugitive slaves in the 1800's, could you use *Caleb's Choice* as a historical source? Why or why not?

Two Views of the War in Kansas

from *America Firsthand*, Vol. I, edited by Robert D. Marcus and David Burner

In 1856, proslavery forces attacked Lawrence, Kansas. An antislavery group led by John Brown attacked Pottawatomie Creek and killed a number of southern settlers. In the following letters, John Lawrie, a northerner, and Axalla John Hoole, a southerner, express their views of the fighting in Kansas.

John Lawrie:

Dear Art,

When I left home on the fifteenth of last June I had no intention of making a home in Kansas. I intended in case I could find any organization ready to take the field against the Missourians [the proslavery settlers], to use my utmost endeavors to change the attitude of the Free-State [antislavery] settlers from a defensive to an offensive warfare. When I reached Leavenworth, I was unable to find any organization of free-state men, and could only tell one when I met him by his hanging head and subdued tone of voice. . . .

Hearing that people held up their heads and spoke what they thought in Lawrence, I started for that point and soon found myself at home as far as a hatred of tyranny and a thirst for vengeance for the insult of the 21st of May was concerned. The people had concluded to try whether there was truth in the Border Ruffian assertion *The . . . Yankees won't fight!* There was quite a stir among the young men in the way of target fighting and drilling in order to prepare themselves for any emergency that might arise requiring them to *contend with superior numbers*, the only thing that thus far has held them back. I found that arms were really scarce. I expected to find plenty of improved firearms, and it was with the greatest difficulty I succeeded in getting an old condemned musket. I was looked upon with distrust by a great many persons in Lawrence, having the appearance of a spy in their eyes. It was complimentary, for my appearance seemed above my position to them; but it was very disagreeable. The only military company in town *(the Stubbs)* expected to attend the convention at Topeka on the second and third of July and the opening of the [antislavery] legislature on the Fourth, when it was expected they would be needed to defend the legislature against the Ruffians and troops of the U.S. I applied for admission into the company and was put off with rather evasive answers. I went up to Topeka, however, resolved to prove myself a true man when the trying time came. I found the people discussing the propriety of defending the legislature against all who might attempt to disperse it. . . .

Axalla John Hoole:

Dear Sister,

I fear, Sister, that coming here will do no good at last, as I begin to think that this will be made a free state at last. 'Tis true we have elected proslavery men to draft a state Constitution, but I feel pretty certain, if it is put to the vote of the people, it will be rejected, as I feel pretty confident they have a majority here at this time. The South has ceased all efforts, while the North is redoubling her exertions. We nominated a candidate for Congress last Friday—Ex-Gov. Ransom of Michigan. I must confess I have not much faith in him, though he professes to hate the abolitionists bitterly, and I have heard him say that Negroes were a great deal better off with masters. Still, I fear him, but it was the best we could do.

endeavors   efforts
vengeance   the act of getting even with someone for a wrong or injury

propriety   agreement with what is proper or fitting or with accepted standards or behavior

Name _____ Date _____

Think It Over

1. What was the point of view of each author on the issue of slavery in Kansas?

2. Why are both of these letters reliable sources of information, even though they are written from opposing points of view?

from *Hospital Sketches*
by Louisa May Alcott

Louisa May Alcott is best known as the author of the classic novel *Little Women.* During the Civil War, Alcott worked at the Union Hospital in the Georgetown area of Washington. She wrote letters home about her experiences as a volunteer nurse. The letters were later published under the title *Hospital Sketches.*

The first thing I met was a regiment of the vilest odors that ever assaulted the human nose . . . and the worst of this affliction was, everyone had assured me that it was a chronic weakness of all hospitals, and I must bear it. I did, armed with lavender water, with which I so besprinkled myself and premises, that, like my friend, Sairy, I was soon known among my patients as "the nurse with the bottle.". . . I progressed by slow stages up stairs and down, till the main hall was reached, and I paused to take breath and a survey. There they were! "our brave boys," as the papers justly call them, for cowards could hardly have been so riddled with shot and shell, so torn and shattered, nor have borne suffering for which we have no name, with an uncomplaining fortitude, which made one glad to cherish each as a brother. In they came, some on stretchers, some in men's arms, some feebly staggering along propped on rude crutches, and one lay stark and still with covered face, as a comrade gave his name to be recorded before they carried him away to the dead house. All was hurry and confusion; the hall was full of these wrecks of humanity, for the most exhausted could not reach a bed till duly ticketed and registered; the walls were lined with rows of such as could sit, the floor covered with the more disabled, the steps and doorways filled with helpers and lookers on; the sound of many feet and voices made that

usually quiet hour as noisy as noon; and, in the midst of it all, the matron's motherly face brought more comfort to many a poor soul, than the cordial draughts she administered, or the cheery words that welcomed all, making of the hospital a home.

The sight of several stretchers, each with its legless, armless, or desperately wounded occupant, entering my ward, admonished me that I was there to work, not to wonder or weep; so I corked up my feelings, and returned to the path of duty, which was rather "a hard road to travel" just then. The house had been a hotel before hospitals were needed, and many of the doors still bore their old names; some not so inappropriate as might be imaged, for my ward was in truth a *ball-room,* if gunshot wounds could christen it. Forty beds were prepared, many already tenanted by tired men who fell down anywhere, and drowsed till the smell of food roused them. Round the great stove was gathered the dreariest group I ever saw—ragged, gaunt and pale, mud to the knees, with bloody bandages untouched since put on days before; many bundled up in blankets, coats being lost or useless; and all wearing that disheartened look which proclaimed defeat. . . . I pitied them so much, I dared not speak to them, though, remembering all they had been through since the roust at Fredericksburg, I yearned to serve the dreariest of them all. Presently, Miss Blank

vilest   most offensive or disgusting
chronic   going on for a long time; constant or habitual
premises   buildings
fortitude   courage to bear up calmly under pain or trouble
feebly   weakly

comrade   fellow soldier
draughts   doses of medicine
admonished   warned to correct some fault; criticized in a mild way
tenanted   occupied

tore me from my refuge behind piles of one-sleeved shirts, odd socks, bandages and lint; put basin, sponge, towels and a block of brown soap into my hands, with these appalling directions:

"Come, my dear, begin to wash as fast as you can. Tell them to take off socks, coats, and shirts, scrub them well, put on clean shirts, and the attendants will finish them off, and lay them in bed."

Think It Over

1. Alcott was writing a letter home to her family. Do you think she included all the details of what she witnessed at the hospital? Why or why not?

The Gettysburg Address
by Abraham Lincoln

At the Battle of Gettysburg in July 1863, the Union army lost more than 23,000 soldiers. The Confederates lost 28,000 men. On November 19, 1863, President Abraham Lincoln visited Gettysburg to dedicate the battlefield cemetery. The brief but stirring speech President Lincoln gave on that day became known as the "Gettysburg Address."

Four score and seven years ago our fathers brought forth on this continent, a new nation, conceived in liberty, and dedicated to the proposition that all men are created equal. Now we are engaged in a great civil war, testing whether that nation, or any nation so conceived and so dedicated, can long endure. We are met on a great battlefield of that war. We have come to dedicate a portion of that field, as a final resting place for those who here gave their lives that that nation might live. It is altogether fitting and proper that we should do this. But, in a larger sense, we can not dedicate—we can not consecrate—we can not hallow—this ground. The brave men, living and dead. who struggled here, have consecrated it, far above our poor power to add or detract. The world will little note, nor long remember what we say here, but it can never forget what they did here. It is for us the living, rather, to be dedicated here to the unfinished work which they who fought here have thus far so nobly advanced. It is rather for us to be here dedicated to the great task remaining before us—that from these honored dead we take increased devotion to that cause for which they gave the last full measure of devotion—that we here highly resolve that these dead shall not have died in vain—that this nation, under God, shall have a new birth of freedom—and that government of the people, by the people, for the people, shall not perish from the earth.

score   twenty (four score means four times twenty, or eighty)
proposition   proposal, plan; here: concept or idea
consecrate   to set apart as holy
hallow   to make or keep holy or sacred
detract   take away
vain   without success or purpose
perish   die

Think It Over

1. Give examples of how Lincoln uses this speech to try to remind people of the ideals upon which the United States was founded.

2. In addition to honoring the dead, is Lincoln trying to gain support for a particular cause? Explain.

A Southerner Looks to the Future
from *Through Some Eventful Years* by Susan Bradford Eppes

Susan Bradford was the daughter of a Florida planter. In November 1866, she married Nicholas Eppes, who had fought in the Confederate army. His family owned a plantation near Tallahassee. Before her marriage, she kept a diary. Later, Susan Bradford Eppes used her diary and her experiences before and after the war to write books about the South.

January 1st, 1866.—A New Year but a Happy New Year? No indeed. We got up this morning to find ourselves the only occupants of Pine Hill plantation. It was a clean sweep, all were gone. . . . Not a servant, not one and we unused to work. . . .

January 2nd, 1866.—I have slept well and I feel decidedly better. I am not going to fret because the negroes are gone, nor will I bother my brains as to their whereabouts. I am going to learn to do all these things that need doing and bye and bye I shall do them well. . . .

February 17th, 1866.—The house party is a thing of the past and will be long remembered. . . . Mrs. Miller is a sweet old lady, a South Carolinian by birth, who married a Northern man. Her invalid son, Lieutenant Charles Miller, excited my pity to such an extent that I have tried to forget his blue [Yankee] uniform and remember only that he suffers. I think the almost constant contact with the sick and wounded soldiers in our own army has automatically made me tender of those who are ill. . . .

Our own boys tease me about my "sick Yankee," but I think it is right or I would not do it. . . .

March 1st, 1866.—Little Diary, I have tried hard to tell you my secret but there are some things too sacred to write about. My Soldier in Gray has held by promise for many months and, before the year is out, we expect to be married. . . .

March 14th, 1866.—Riding horse-back with My Soldier this afternoon I told him . . .

I had heard Mr. Coolidge [a Yankee officer] was related to him and if that was so I wanted to know why he did not make friends with him? He looked very serious and I was beginning to fear I had hurt him in some unknown way.

At last he spoke, "I have never mentioned my cousin, Sidney Coolidge to you; he came to Florida to visit our family prior to the war. . . . I loved my cousin Sidney and looked forward to the visit, which he had promised us at some future time.

"The war came on and during the whole four years of war, I was in the thickest of the fighting. After Gettysburg I was promoted and assigned to the Army of the West. One day I was sent to carry a dispatch for my general. Crossing the field of Chickamauga, I was hit by a bullet; . . . I was stunned but soon recovered, delivered the dispatch and turned to go. An officer who knew me, laid his hand on my arm and said:

" 'Your cousin, Colonel Coolidge, lies dead in that tent, don't you want to go and look at him?'. . . .

"Now, this young lieutenant you like so much, is probably a relative . . . but this is the way I feel about it; if the Confederates had been the victorious army and I had been occupying the conquered country, if, in fact, our positions could be reversed, I should look him up, claim the tie of blood and proffer the hand of friendship. As things stand, he is the conqueror, I am the conquered and if any advances are made they must come from him. . . ."

July 21st, 1866.—This is the anniversary of the Battle of Manassas. How

fret become worried
invalid not well; weak and sick

dispatch an official message
proffer offer

hopeful we were then and it seems ages ago, so much has crowded into life in these last years. . . .

August 26th, 1866.—We have to look ahead and plan for the fall wedding which My Soldier pleads for. . . . I do not want a grand wedding such as my sisters had; circumstances are so different now. Father's fortune has been swept away by the results of the war. It is true, he still has his land but that is almost valueless at present and it may never bring in anything again as land without labor is a poor proposition.

Father has aged since the surrender and he will never be able to recoup his losses. All this show and expense is wholly unnecessary.What I would like would be a pretty wedding dress, every girl wants that, but I

want a quiet wedding with my family and his family present and some of his friends and some of my friends for attendants. . . .

October 5th, 1866.—My dress has been bought. . . . [Mother] has let all our friends know that "no wedding presents must be sent." She says the South is impoverished, there are few who can afford to give a handsome gift and yet almost every one will spend that which they can ill-afford, rather than be outdone in general giving. I am well satisfied with this arrangement. . . .

November 1st, 1866.—My dear little friend . . . I am telling you goodbye. Whatever the future may bring me of weal or woe will not be recorded. This is My Day, my wedding day.

proposition plan
recoup to make up for

impoverished very poor

Think It Over

1. How does Susan Bradford Eppes reveal her feelings about the South after the war?

2. Eppes did not publish her diary at the time it was written. She selected certain passages to include in a book nearly 60 years later. What information would help you judge the reliability of the published diary as a source of information?

from *Out From This Place*
by Joyce Hansen

Out From This Place by Joyce Hansen is a novel about African American life at the start of Reconstruction. In the final chapter, Easter, a freed slave, writes a letter to Miss Grantley, the woman who taught her how to read. Easter describes what she finally decided to do with her life. The letter also describes what life was like for freedmen in a small South Carolina town.

March 31, 1866

Dear Miss Grantley,

I hope this letter finds you enjoying the best of health. Please forgive me for taking so long to write to you, but it took me this long to make another decision. First, let me tell you how our town is coming along. We call it New Canaan. We have a church, a school, and we are building a molasses mill and a general store. Some of the people still work for the Williams family to make extra money for the land they purchased.

Miss Fortune moved to the cabin that was built next to the school especially for the teacher. We call it the teacher's house. The men and women take turns keeping guard, though, to make certain that the buckra don't come and burn down our school as they try to do last week. Miss Fortune smelled the smoke and saw the men who set the fire riding away. She say it looked like they was wearing some kind of hood. Thank God we put the fire out before it made much damage. And to think we told her to come and live among us because we thought she would be safer with us than in the cottage near the big house!

Some bad news. Miriam and several other children died from a terrible fever. Brother Thomas still cannot talk and cannot walk by himself. But we pray that one day he'll be better.

Now for my life. I have decided, first, not to marry Julius but to go back to the old Rebel camp and find Mariah and Gabriel. Remember I tell you about them? If Obi is searching for me, he'll go to them because that's where he last left me. I went to the Freedmen's Bureau even though I said I wasn't going again, and I was told that they have a list from a colored regiment. They will write to me when they get more information.

Jason joined a medicine show. I got a letter from him and he says he is happy and fine. I miss him so much.

Now for the big news and decision: I want to go to the school in Philadelphia. We don't have enough schools or teachers to go around. Our small schoolhouse is full to overflowing, with some of the children coming from the Riverview plantation. Rose and Miss Fortune helped me to make up my mind to go to Philadelphia. Also, Miss Fortune said that I could live with her family while I attended the school. That made me feel less afraid about going. I have a welcome letter from her family already saying that I do not have to worry about my room and board.

So, my dear Miss Grantley, I hope you are happy and excited about my decision as I am. I hope it's not too late for me to attend the school. I saved a little bit of money, and Rose and a few of the other people want to help pay some of the costs too. I look forward to hearing from you soon. I am, as always,

Your Friend and Student,
Easter

Think It Over

1. Based on this reading, what impression does the author want to create about freed slaves in the South during Reconstruction?

2. Could you use this letter as an authentic historical document about Reconstruction in the South? Why or why not?

from *A Century of Dishonor*
by Helen Hunt Jackson

After Helen Hunt Jackson attended a lecture on the problems of the Native Americans, she began to research the government's mistreatment of them. In 1881, she published *A Century of Dishonor,* based on her research. The book exposes the many abuses suffered by Native Americans. As a result, Jackson was appointed to a federal commission investigating the condition of Indians living on missions. She also wrote *Ramona,* a popular novel about Indians in California. The following excerpt is from *A Century of Dishonor.*

There is not among these three hundred bands of Indians [in the United States] one which has not suffered cruelly at the hands either of the government or of white settlers. The poorer, the more insignificant, the more helpless the band, the more certain the cruelty and outrage to which they have been subjected. This especially true of the bands on the Pacific slopes. These Indians found themselves of a sudden surrounded by and caught up in the great influx of gold-seeking settlers, as helpless creatures on a shore are caught up in a tidal wave. There was not time for the government to make laws. The tale of the wrongs, the oppressions, the murders of the Pacific-slope Indians in the last thirty years would be a volume by itself, and is too monstrous to be believed.

It makes little difference, however, where one opens the record of the history of the Indians; every page and every year has its dark stain. The story of one tribe is the story of all, varied only by differences of time and place; but neither time nor place makes any difference in the main facts. Colorado is as greedy and unjust in 1880 as was Georgia in 1830, and Ohio in 1795; and the United States government breaks promises now as deftly as then, and with added ingenuity from long practice.

One of its strongest supports in doing so is the widespread sentiment among the peo-ple of dislike to the Indian, of impatience with his presence as a "barrier to civiliza-tion," and distrust of it as a possible danger. The old tales of the frontier life, with its hor-rors of Indian warfare, have gradually, by two or three generations' telling, produced in the average mind something like an hereditary instinct of unquestioning and unreasoning aversion which it is almost impossible to dislodge or soften.

There are hundreds of pages of unimpeachable testimony on the side of the Indian; but it goes for nothing, is set down as sentimentalism or partisanship, tossed aside and forgotten.

President after President has appointed commission after commission to inquire into and report upon Indian affairs, and to make suggestions as to the best methods of managing them. The reports are filled with eloquent statements of wrongs done to the Indians. . . . These reports are bound up with the Government's Annual Report, and that it is the end of them. . . .

In 1869 President Grant appointed a commission of nine men, representing the influence and philanthropy of six leading States, to visit the different Indian reserva-tions, and to "examine all matters [relating] to Indian affairs."

In the report of the commission are such paragraphs as the following.

influx   a coming in without stopping
deftly   quickly and surely; skillfully
ingenuity   cleverness
hereditary   inherited from an ancestor
aversion   a strong dislike
unimpeachable   that cannot be doubted, questioned or discredited

partisanship   strong loyalty toward a particular group, cause, or political party
eloquent   stirring people's feelings or having an effect on how they think
philanthropy   goodwill toward others

"To assert that 'the Indian will not work' is as true as it would be to say that the white man will not work.

"Why should the Indian be expected to plant corn, fence lands, build houses, or do anything but get food from day to day, when experience had taught him that the product of his labor will be seized by the white man tomorrow? The most industrious white man would become a drone under similar circumstances. Nevertheless, many of the Indians" (the commissioners might more forcibly have said 130,000 of the Indians) "are already at work, and furnish ample refutation of the assertion that 'the Indian will not work.' There is no escape from the . . . logic of facts.

"The history of the government connection with the Indians is a shameful record of broken treaties and unfulfilled promises. The history of the border, white man's connection with the Indians is a sickening record of murder, outrage, robbery, and wrongs committed by the former, as the rule, and occasional savage outbreaks and unspeakable barbarous deeds of retaliation by the latter, as the exception.

"Taught by the government that they had rights entitled to respect, when those rights have been assailed by the rapacity of the white man, the arm which should have been raised to protect them has ever been ready to sustain the aggressor." . . .

However great perplexity and difficulty there may be in the details of any and every plan possible for doing at this late day anything like justice to the Indian, however hard it may be for good statesmen and good men to agree upon the things that ought to be done, there certainly is, or ought to be, no perplexity whatever, no difficulty whatever, in agreeing upon certain things that ought not to be done, and which must cease to be done before the first steps can be taken toward righting the wrongs, curing the ills, and wiping out the disgrace to us of the present condition of our Indians.

Cheating, robbing, breaking promises— these three are clearly things which must cease to be done. One more thing, also, and that is the refusal of the protection of the law to the Indian's rights of property, "of life, liberty, and the pursuit of happiness."

When these four things have ceased to be done, time, statesmanship, philanthropy, and Christianity can slowly and surely do the rest. Till these four things have ceased to be done, statesmanship and philanthropy alike must work in vain, and even Christianity can reap but small harvest.

drone a person who does hard, tedious work
refutation a reason or argument that proves something wrong or false

rapacity greed

Think It Over

1. Did Jackson base *A Century of Dishonor* on her own first-hand observations? If not, on what did she base it?

2. What facts does Helen Hunt Jackson use to support her position on Native American rights?

Eyewitness Account ★★★★★★
GEOGRAPHY

from *From the Pecos to the Powder: A Cowboy's Autobiography*
by Bob Kennon

In the following selection, Bob Kennon describes working on long cattle drives from Mexico to Montana in the late 1800's.

Don Luis Terrazas, the cattle king of Chihuahua, was the largest landholder and cattle breeder in the world at the time. He owned about 1,000,000 head of cattle and branded as high as 200,000 calves in one year at one time. Before the revolution later broke him, he had over 3,000 head of horses in use on his more than 11,000,000 acres of ranches.

Bill Nort, one of the foremen, gave me a job wrangling horses. He was a kindly sort of man who understood and could talk with a kid like me. Taking this job was the turning point of my life. I had only been working there a few months when Mr. Broadus and Mr. Hysham, two cowmen from Montana, together with their foreman, Mr. Baker, came down to buy steers.

They bought two thousand Mexican steers from Terrazzas, and Baker was to trail north to Montana. Baker asked Bill Nort and Tom Cottrell, a Terrazas cowhand, myself, and a few others to come along up the trail. I was willing and anxious to go up the cattle trail at any time. This had been my hope and dream for months. If a fellow had never been up to Montana on a cattle drive, he wasn't considered much of a cowman. I held back, though, until Mr. Broadus agreed to pay me a monthly wage of forty dollars for the trip. Compared with the eighteen dollars I was getting, this seemed like a fortune to me and I told him I'd go all the way.

At last everything was in readiness, the cattle gathered, tallied, and turned over to Broadus with Hysham. With the transaction closed, the wagons loaded with supplies, beds, etc., and the cook fixed out with all his culinary needs, everything was complete for the long trip north. The remuda of horses was gathered, and every cowhand had his own saddle, chaps, and war-bag where he kept his personal belongings.

Early the next morning we crossed the Rio Grande under Terrazas' supervision. After crossing into Texas, Broadus and Hysham gave the orders. We didn't travel fast nor very far in a week's time, and camped at regular intervals, holding the steers on good feed all along the way. Cattle get footsore and leg weary if crowded too hard or handled roughly, and they wanted the steers to reach Montana in good condition. . . .

The trail itself, as I've said, was well planned for us. It lay across the tablelands, or mesas, of West Texas and into Kansas, crossed part of the Old Santa Fe Trail near Dodge City, then led onward to the North Platte, keeping clear of Ogallala, that big cow town full of fun and trouble for a bunch of cowboys on a trail drive. We skirted the Black Hills and went on into Montana. We varied somewhat in later drives as herd men found it was far better to avoid all towns unless there were stockyards there. At any rate, these shipping places were nearly all at a distance outside the towns themselves.

We unloaded the steers for the last time at Wichita, Kansas, and took them on across Kansas by trail, then across the North Platte River and the sand hills of Nebraska. On northwest of Deadwood, South Dakota, we traveled for about forty or fifty miles, going by Devil's Tower and the Belle Fourche country. Belle Fourche was a cowman's country

wrangling   rounding up in a herd
culinary   having to do with cooking
remuda   a group of extra saddle horses kept as a supply of remounts

chaps   leather trousers without a seat, worn over ordinary trousers by cowboys to protect their legs

in the brakes of the Little Missouri where there was an abundance of fine feed.

We were getting excited by this time. No one seemed tired any more. In our minds we were already spending our pay in Miles City, and nothing could dampen our spirits. We were getting mighty tired of looking at those steers, and yet we had come so far together they seemed like old friends.

We came on down Little Cottonwood and at last crossed the Powder River. We were sure happy at the sight of it, and if we hadn't been trailing those two thousand steers and afraid of stampeding them, we'd have shot into the air to celebrate our arrival, for every cowman's slogan was "Powder River or bust." Though we'd been in Montana for several days, no one could really believe it until we had crossed the Powder.

After crossing, we went over to the Broadus holdings, which were in close on the other side. The town of Broadus was established here on the old site of this ranch. We crossed the Little Powder at the Half Circle Cross Ranch, then went down the Mitzpah and on to Miles City. We were now nearing the end of our long trail and coming to the beautiful Yellowstone River. . . . We swam the herd and remuda across the Yellowstone while the wagons were ferried across, and our job was done.

ferried   transported across a river

Think It Over

1. How did Bob Kennon view the job of a cowboy on the cattle drive?

2. Did Kennon write this account soon after this cattle drive or years later? How can you tell?

from *The Empire of Business*
by Andrew Carnegie

Andrew Carnegie was a self-made man. He became a successful steel manufacturer and philanthropist. The following selection is from a talk Carnegie gave to students at a business school in Pittsburgh in 1885. Carnegie advises students about how to succeed in business.

It is well that young men should begin at the beginning and occupy the most subordinate positions. Many of the leading businessmen of Pittsburgh had a serious responsibility thrust upon them at the very threshold of their career. They were introduced to the broom, and spent the first hours of their business lives sweeping out the office. I notice we have janitors and janitresses now in offices, and our young men unfortunately miss that salutary branch of a business education. But if by chance the professional sweeper is absent any morning the boy who has the genius of the future partner in him will not hesitate to try his hand at the broom. . . .

[T]he question now is how to rise from the subordinate position we have imagined you in, through the successive grades to the position for which you are, in my opinion, and, I trust, in your own, evidently intended. I can give you the secret. It lies mainly in this. Instead of the question, "What must I do for my employer?" substitute "What can I do?" Faithful and conscientious discharge of the duties assigned you is all very well, but the verdict in such cases generally is that you perform your present duties so well that you had better continue performing them. Now, young gentlemen, this will not do. It will not do for the coming partners. There must be something beyond this. We make clerks, bookkeepers, treasurers, bank tellers of this class, and there they remain to the end of the chapter. The rising man must do something exceptional, and beyond the range of his special department. He must attract attention. A shipping clerk, he may do so by discovering in an invoice an error with which he has nothing to do, and which has escaped the attention of the proper party. If a weighing clerk, he may save for the firm by doubting the adjustment of the scales and having them corrected, even if this be the province of the master mechanic. If a messenger boy, even he can lay the seed of promotion by going beyond the letter of his instructions in order to secure the desired reply. There is no service so low and simple, neither any so high, in which the young man of ability and willing disposition cannot readily and almost daily prove himself capable of greater trust and usefulness, and, what is equally important, show his invincible determination to rise. Some day, in your own department, you will be directed to do or say something which you know will prove disadvantageous to the interest of the firm. Here is your chance. Stand up like a man and say so. Say it boldly, and give your reasons, and thus prove to your employer that, while his thoughts have been engaged upon other matters, you have been studying during hours when perhaps he thought you asleep, how to advance his interests. You may be right or you may be wrong, but in either case you have gained the first condition of success. You have attracted attention. Your employer has found that he has not a mere hireling in his service, but a man; not one who is content to give so many hours of work for so many dollars in return, but one who devotes his spare hours and constant thought to the business. Such an employee must perforce be thought of, and thought of kindly and well. It will not be long before his advice is asked in his special branch, and if the advice given be sound, it will soon be asked and taken upon questions of broader bearing. This means partnership; if not with present employers then

subordinate low in rank
salutary useful or helpful

perforce because it must be; necessarily

with others. Your foot, in such a case, is upon the ladder; the amount of climbing done depends entirely [on] yourself. . . . There is one sure mark of the coming partner, the future millionaire: his revenues always exceed his expenditures. He begins to save early, almost as soon as he begins to earn. No matter how little it may be possible to save, save that little. Invest it securely, not necessarily in bonds, but in anything which you have good reason to believe will be profitable, but no gambling with it, remember. A rare chance will soon present itself for investment. The little you have saved will prove the basis for an amount of credit utterly surprising to you. Capitalists trust the saving young man. For every hundred dollars you can produce as the result of hard-won savings, [a rich man], in search of partner, will lend or credit a thousand; for every thousand, fifty thousand. It is not capital that your seniors require, it is the man who has proved that he has the business

habits which create capital, and to create it in the best of all possible ways, as far as self-discipline is concerned, is, by adjusting his habits to his means. Gentlemen, it is the first hundred dollars saved which tells. Begin at once to [save] up something. The bee predominates in the future millionaire.

Of course there are better, higher aims than saving. As an end, the acquisition of wealth is ignoble to the extreme; I assume that you save and long for wealth only as a means of enabling you the better to do some good in your day and generation. Make a note of this essential rule: Expenditure always within income. . . .

To summarize what I have said: Aim for the highest . . . make the firm's interest yours; break orders always to save owners; concentrate; put all your eggs in one basket, and watch that basket; expenditure always within revenue; lastly, be not impatient, for, as Emerson says, "no one can cheat you out of ultimate success but yourself."

revenues   money that is taken in
expenditures   money that is spent

predominates   has greatest power; dominates
ignoble   not honorable; shameful

Think It Over

1. Summarize Carnegie's view of how young men can succeed.

2. Why would young people of 1885 be likely to listen to Carnegie's advice about business?

from *America Firsthand*, Vol. II
edited by Robert D. Marcus and David Burner

On March 25, 1911, a fire broke out in the shop of the Triangle Shirtwaist Company. The company was located on the eighth, ninth, and tenth floors of a "fireproof" building in New York City. In this selection, Pauline Newman, a former Triangle Shirtwaist Company worker, tells what it was like to work there. An article from the *New York World* newspaper then describes the fire.

Pauline Newman

I'd like to tell you about the kind of world we lived in 75 years ago because all of you probably weren't even born then. Seventy-five years is a long time, but I'd like to give you at least a glimpse of that world because it has no resemblance to the world we live in today, in any respect.

That world 75 years ago was a world of incredible exploitation of men, women, and children. I went to work for the Triangle Shirtwaist Company in 1901. The corner of a shop would resemble a kindergarten because we were young, eight, nine, ten years old. It was a world of greed; the human being didn't mean anything. The hours were from 7:30 in the morning to 6:30 at night when it wasn't busy. . . . You would go home, what kind of home did you go to? You won't find the tenements we lived in. Some of the rooms didn't have any windows. I lived in a two room tenement with my mother and two sisters and the bedroom had no windows, the facilities were down in the yard, but that's the way it was in the factories too. In the summer the sidewalk, fire escapes, and the roof of the tenements became bedrooms just to get a breath of air.

We wore cheap clothes, lived in cheap tenements, ate cheap food. There was nothing to look forward to, nothing to expect the next day to be better.

Someone once asked me; "How did you survive?" And I told him, what alternative did we have? You stayed and you survived, that's all.

negligence carelessness

The New York World

At 4:35 o'clock yesterday afternoon fire springing from a source that may never be positively identified was discovered in the rear of the eighth floor of the ten story building at the northwest corner of Washington Place and Greene Street, the first of three floors occupied as a factory of the Triangle Shirtwaist Company.

At 11:30 o'clock Chief Croker made this statement:

"Everybody has been removed. The number taken out, which includes those who jumped from windows, is 141. . . ."

At 2 o'clock this morning Chief Croker estimated the total dead as one hundred and fifty-four. He said further: "I expect something of this kind to happen in these so-called fire-proof buildings, which are without adequate protection as far as fire-escapes are concerned. . . ."

Inspection by Acting Superintendent of Buildings Ludwig will be made the basis for charges of criminal negligence on the ground that the fire-proof doors leading to one of the enclosed tower stairways were locked. . . .

Before smoke or flame gave signs from the windows, the loss of life was fully under way. The first signs that persons in the street knew that these three top stories had turned into red furnaces in which human creatures were being caught and incinerated was when screaming men and women and boys and girls crowded out on the many window ledges and threw themselves into the streets far below. . . .

incinerated burned up

Some, about seventy, chose a successful avenue of escape. They clambered up a ladder to the roof. A few remembered the fire escape. Many may have thought of it but only as they uttered cries of dismay.

Wretchedly inadequate was this fire escape—a lone ladder running down to a rear narrow court, which was smoke filled as the fire raged, one narrow door giving access to the ladder. By the score they fought and struggled and breathed fire and died trying to make that needle-eye road to self-preservation. . . .

Concentrated, the fire burned within. The flames caught all the flimsy lace stuff and linens that go into the making of spring and summer shirtwaists and fed eagerly upon rolls of silk.

The cutting room was laden with stuff on long tables. The employees were toiling over such material at the rows and rows of machines. Sinisterly the spring day gave aid to the fire. Many of the window panes facing south and east were drawn down. Drafts had full play.

The experts say that the three floors must each have become a whirlpool of fire. Whichever way the entrapped creatures fled they met a curving sweep of flame. Many swooned and died. Others fought their way to the windows or the elevator or fell fighting for a chance at the fire escape, the single fire escape leading into the blind court that was to be reached from the upper floors by clambering over a window sill!

On all three floors, at a narrow window, a crowd met death trying to get out to that one slender fire escape ladder.

It was a fireproof building in which this enormous tragedy occurred. Save for the three stories of blackened windows at the top, you would scarcely have been able to tell where the fire had happened. The walls stood firmly. A thin tongue of flame now and then licked around a window sash. . . .

clambered   climbed with effort, using the hands as well as the feet
inadequate   less than is needed

toiling   working hard
sinisterly   most unfortunately

Think It Over

1. You have just read two types of primary sources: a first-person account and a newspaper report. Compare what kinds of information you can get from these two types of sources.

from *Coming to America*
edited by Katherine Emsden

from *The American Reader,*
edited by Diane Ravitch

In the late 1800's, numerous Europeans and Asians immigrated to the United States. Europeans arrived at Ellis Island in New York City. Asians arrived at Angel Island in San Francisco. Angel Island was used as an entry point for Asian immigrants awaiting admission and as a detention center for those awaiting deportation. The first two selections are the recollections of European immigrants. They describe their experiences of trying to make a living in an American city. The other selection is a poem written by an Asian immigrant who was detained on Angel Island.

An Italian Immigrant:

. . . We came to Brooklyn, New York, to a wooden house in Adams Street that was full of Italians from Naples. Bartolo had a room on the third floor and there were fifteen men in the room, all boarding with Bartolo. He did the cooking on a stove in the middle of the room and there were beds all around the sides, one bed above another. It was very hot in the room, but we were soon asleep, for we were very tired.

The next morning, early, Bartolo told us to go out and pick rags and get bottles. He gave us bags and hooks and showed us the ash barrels. On the streets where the fine houses are the people are very careless and put out good things, like mattresses and umbrellas, clothes, bats, and boots. We brought all these to Bartolo and he made them new again and sold them on the sidewalk; but mostly we brought rags and bones. The rags we had to wash in the backyard and then we hung them to dry on lines under the ceiling in our room. The bones we kept under the beds till Bartolo could find a man to buy them.

Most of the men in our room worked at digging the sewer. Bartolo got them work and they paid him about one-quarter of their wages. Then he charged them for board and he bought the clothes for them, too. So they got little money after all.

Bartolo was always saying that the rent of the room was so high that he could not make anything, but he was really making plenty. . . and is now a very rich man.

A Lithuanian Immigrant:

. . . [In Lithuania you paid] with sacks of rye. But here you want a hundred things. Whenever you walk out you see new things you want, and you must have money to buy everything. . . .

The next morning my friends woke me at five o'clock and said, "Now, if you want life, liberty, and happiness," they laughed, "you must push for yourself. You must get a job. Come with us." And we went to the [Chicago stock] yards. Men and women were walking in by thousands as far as we could see. We went to the doors of one big slaughterhouse. There was a crowd of about 200 men waiting there for a job. They looked hungry and kept watching the door. At last a special policeman came out and began pointing to men, one by one. Each one jumped forward. Twenty-three were taken. Then they all went outside, and all the others turned their faces away and looked tired. I remember one boy sat down and cried, just next to me, on a pile of boards. Some policemen waved their clubs and we all walked on. I found some Lithuanians to talk with, who told me they had come every morning for three weeks. Soon we met other crowds coming away from other slaughterhouses, and we all walked around and felt bad and tired and hungry.

That night I told my friends that I would not do this many days, but would go some place else. "Where?" they asked me, and I began to see then that I was in bad trouble, because I spoke no English. Then one man told me to give him $5 to give the special policeman. I did this and the next morning the policeman pointed me out, so I had a job. The union is doing another good thing. It is combining all the nationalities. The night I joined the Cattle Butchers' Union I was led into the room by a negro member. With me were Bohemians, Germans and Poles, and Mike Donnelly, the President, is an Irishman.

Poem From Angel Island:

I used to admire the land of the Flowery
    Flag* as a country of abundance.

_____

*Flowery Flag refers to the colorful flag of the United States.

sojourn   a short stay
ordeals   difficult and painful experiences

I immediately raised money and started my
    journey.
For over a month, I have experienced enough
    winds and waves.
Now on an extended sojourn in jail, I am
    subject to the ordeals of prison life.
I look up and see Oakland so close by.
I wish to go back to my motherland to carry
    the farmer's hoe.
Discontent fills my belly and it is difficult for
    me to sleep.
I just write these few lines to express what is
    on my mind.

discontent   a feeling of not being satisfied and of wanting something different

Think It Over

1. The first two excerpts come from a series of interviews by a reporter in the early 1900's. He spoke to several immigrants, and then published the interviews in a newspaper. Why is it important to know these facts when you evaluate this source?

2. In the poem from Angel Island, how does the writer view the United States?

Suffrage for Women
by Carrie Chapman Catt

In the early 1900's, Carrie Chapman Catt became the head of the National American Woman Suffrage Association (NAWSA). The following excerpt is from Chapman's speech to the NAWSA in February 1902.

The question of woman suffrage is a very simple one. The plea is dignified, calm, and logical. Yet, great as is the victory over conservatism which is represented in the accomplishment of man suffrage, infinitely greater will be the attainment of woman suffrage. Man suffrage exists through the surrender of many a stronghold of ancient thought. . . .

Woman suffrage must meet precisely the same objections which have been urged against man suffrage, but in addition, it must combat sex-prejudice, the oldest, the most unreasoning, the most stubborn of all human idiosyncrasies. What is prejudice? An opinion, which is not based upon reason; a judgment, without having heard the argument; a feeling, without being able to trace whence it came. And sex-prejudice is a pre-judgment against the rights, liberties, and opportunities of women. A belief, without proof, in the incapacity of women to do that which they have never done. Sex-prejudice has been the chief hindrance in the rapid advance of the woman's rights movement to its present status, and still a stupendous obstacle to be overcome. . . .

Four chief causes led to the subjection of women, each the logical deduction from the theory that men were the units of the race—obedience, ignorance, the denial of personal liberty and the denial of right to property and wages. These forces united in cultivating a spirit of egotism and tyranny in men and weak dependence in women. . . . In fastening these disabilities upon women, the world acted logically when reasoning from the premise that man is the race and woman his dependent. The perpetual tutelage and subjection robbed women of all freedom of thought and action, and all incentive for growth, and they logically became the inane weaklings the world would have them, and their condition strengthened the universal belief in their incapacity. This world taught woman nothing skillful and then said her work was valueless. It permitted her no opinions and said she did not know how to think. It forbade her to speak in public, and said the sex had no orators. It denied her the schools, and said the sex had no genius. It robbed her of every vestige of responsibility, and then called her weak. . . .

Shall the woman who enjoys the right of self-government in every other department of life be permitted the right of self-government in the state? It is no more right for all men to govern all women than it was for one man to govern one woman. It is no more right for men to govern women than it was for one man to govern other men.

suffrage the right to vote in political elections
idiosyncrasies unusual or peculiar ways of behaving
incapacity lack of ability or fitness
egotism selfishness

tyranny very cruel and unjust use of power
premise a statement or belief that is takes for granted and is used as the basis for a theory
perpetual tutelage constant teaching

Think It Over

1. What do you think Catt meant by the statement "It is no more right for men to govern women than it was for one man to govern other men"?

2. Was Carrie Chapman Catt speaking to an audience who shared her viewpoint? How might this have affected what she said?

from *Up From Slavery*
by Booker T. Washington

In the 1890's, African Americans living in both the North and South faced many obstacles. In his book *Up From Slavery,* Booker T. Washington argued that before African Americans could attain political or social equality, they needed to acquire education and job training. In the following selection from *Up From Slavery,* Washington writes about his ideas for African American education.

The years from 1867 to 1878 I think may be called the period of Reconstruction. This included the time that I spent at Hampton and as a teacher in West Virginia. During the whole of the Reconstruction period two ideas were constantly agitating the minds of the colored people, or, at least, the minds of a large part of the race. One of these was the craze for Greek and Latin learning, and the other was a desire to hold office.

It could not have been expected that a people who had spent generations in slavery, and before that generations in the darkest heathenism, could at first form any proper conception of what an education meant. In every part of the South, during the Reconstruction period, schools, both day and night, were filled to overflowing with people of all ages and conditions, some being as far along in age as sixty and seventy years. The ambition to secure an education was most praiseworthy and encouraging. The idea, however, was too prevalent that, as soon as one secured a little education, in some unexplainable way he would be free from most of the hardships of the world, and, at any rate, could live without manual labor. There was a further feeling that a knowledge, however little, of the Greek and Latin languages would make one a very superior human being. . . . I remember that the first colored man whom I saw who knew something about foreign languages impressed me at that time as being a man of all others to be envied.

Naturally, most of our people who received some little education became teachers or preachers. While among these two classes there were many capable, earnest, godly men and women, still a large propor-

tion took up teaching or preaching as an easy way to make a living. Many became teachers who could do little more than write their names. . . .

During the whole of the Reconstruction period our people throughout the South looked to the federal government for everything. . . . This was not unnatural. The central government gave them freedom, and the whole nation had been enriched for more than two centuries by the labor of the Negro. Even as a youth, and later in manhood, I had the feeling that it was cruelly wrong in the central government, at the beginning of our freedom, to fail to make some provision for the general education of our people in addition to what the states might do, so that the people would be better prepared for the duties of citizenship. . . .

During the time I was a student in Washington, the city was crowded with colored people, many of whom had recently come from the South. A large proportion of these people had been drawn to Washington because they felt that they could lead a life of ease there. Others had secured minor government positions, and still another large class was there in the hope of securing federal positions. All this tended to make Washington an attractive place for members of the colored race. Then, too, they knew that at all times they could have the protection of the law in the District of Columbia. The public schools in Washington for colored people were better then they were elsewhere. I took great interest in studying the life of our people there closely at that time. . . .

In Washington I saw girls whose mothers were earning their living by laundering.

prevalent   common

These girls were taught by their mothers, in a rather crude way it is true, the industry of laundering. Later these girls entered the public schools and remained there perhaps six or eight years. When the public school course was finally finished, they wanted more costly dresses, more costly hats and shoes. In a word, while their wants had been increased, their ability to supply their wants had not been increased in the same degree. On the other hand, their six or eight years of book education had weaned them away from the occupations of their mothers. The result of this was too many cases that the girls went to the bad. I often thought how much wiser it would have been to give these girls the same amount of mental training—and I favor any kind of training, whether in the languages or mathematics, that gives strength and culture to the mind—but at the same time to give them the most thorough training in the latest and best methods of laundering and other kindred occupations.

Think It Over

1. What kind of education did Booker T. Washington favor? Why?

A Japanese Mission to the United States
from *The Autobiography Yukichi Fukuzawa*

In 1854, Matthew Perry forced Japan to open two ports to trade. Four years later, Japan sent its first mission to the United States. Among the visitors was Yukichi Fukuzawa. He had learned English and was eager to study western ways. Fukuzawa toured the United States, and later he visited Europe. Back home, he wrote articles and books explaining Western ideas and practices to the Japanese. This selection is from Fukuzawa's *Autobiography.* It recalls his impressions of his first days in San Francisco.

As soon as our ship came into the port of San Francisco, we were greeted by many important personages who came on board from all over the country. Along the shores thousands of people were lined up to see the strange newcomers. . . .

As soon as we came on shore, we found we were to be driven off in carriages to a hotel. While we were resting in the hotel, city officials and various dignitaries came to offer entertainment. We were given quarters in the official residence of the Navy station on Mare Island. Our hosts knew that we Japanese were accustomed to a different diet, so they arranged that our food, instead of being served, should be prepared by our own cook. But the officials being very kind, and desiring to satisfy the Japanese love for seafood, sent fish every day. Also, on learning the Japanese custom of bathing frequently, they had baths prepared daily. Our ship had been damaged by the passing storms, so it was put in dry dock to be repaired—all expressions of American hospitality. This generous treatment in every way brought to mind an old expression of ours—"as if our host had put us on the palm of his hand to see that we lacked nothing."

On our part there were many confusing and embarrassing moments, for we were quite ignorant of the customs of American life. For instance, we were surprised even by the carriages. On seeing a vehicle with horses attached to it, we should easily have guessed what it was. But really we did not identify our mode of conveyance until the

door had been opened, we were seated inside, and the horses had started off. Then we realized we were riding in a carriage behind horses.

All of us wore the usual pair of swords at our sides and the hemp [rope] sandals. So attired, we were taken to the modern hotel. There we noticed, covering the interior, the valuable carpets which in Japan only the more wealthy could buy from importers' shops at so much a square inch to make purses and tobacco pouches with. Here the carpet was laid over an entire room— something quite astounding—upon this costly fabric walked our hosts wearing the shoes with which they had come in from the streets! . . .

One evening our hosts said that some ladies and gentlemen were having a dancing party and that they would be glad to have us attend it. We went. To our dismay we could not make out what they were doing. The ladies and gentlemen seemed to be hopping about the room together. As funny as it was, we knew it would be rude to laugh, and we controlled our expressions with difficulty as the dancing went on. These were but a few of the instances of our bewilderment at the strange customs of American society.

When we were taking leave, our host and hostess kindly offered us horses to ride home on. This pleased us, for a chance to ride horseback again was a relief. Especially did Captain Kimura enjoy this, for he was an accomplished horseman who used to ride every day in Yedo. We touched whip to the

personages people
dignitaries persons holding high positions in the government

dry dock a dock from which the water can be emptied
conveyance transportation
bewilderment the fact or condition of being confused

horses and rode back to our quarters at a trot. The Americans watched us and exclaimed at the Japanese ability in riding. So neither of us really knew much about the other after all.

Our hosts in San Francisco were very considerate in showing us examples of modern industry. There was as yet no railway laid to the city, nor was there any electric light in use. But the telegraph system and also Galvani's electroplating were already in use. Then we were taken to a sugar refinery and had the principle of the operation explained to us quite minutely [in detail]. I am sure that our hosts thought they were showing us something entirely new, naturally looking for our surprise at each new device of modern engineering. But on the contrary, there was really nothing new, at least to me. I knew the principle of telegraphy even if I had not seen the actual machine before; I knew that sugar was bleached by straining the solution with bone-black, and that in boiling down the solution, the vacuum was used to better effect than heat. I had been studying nothing else but such scientific principles ever since I had entered Ogata's school.

Rather, I was suprised by entirely different things in American life. First of all, there seemed to be an enormous waste of iron everywhere. In garbage piles on the seashores—everywhere—I found lying old oil tins, empty cans, and broken tools. This was remarkable to us, for in Yedo [today Tokyo], after a fire, there would appear a swarm of people looking for nails in the ashes.

Then too, I was surprised at the high cost of daily commodities in California. We had to pay a half-dollar for a bottle of oysters, and there were only twenty or thirty in the bottle at that. In Japan the price of so many would be only a cent or two.

Things social, political, and economic proved most inexplicable. One day, on a sudden thought, I asked a gentleman where the descendants of George Washington might be. He replied, "I think there is a woman who is directly descended from Washington. I don't know where she is now, but I think I have heard she is married." His answer was so very casual that it shocked me.

Of course, I knew that America was a republic with a new president every four years, but I could not help feeling that the family of Washington would be revered above all other families. My reasoning was based on the reverence in Japan for the founders of the great lines of rulers. . . .

refinery a place where the sugar is purified
commodities articles of trade

inexplicable impossible to explain or understand
revered loved and respected greatly

Think It Over

1. Why did Fukuzawa expect Americans to treat the descendants of George Washington with great respect?

from *Culebra Cut*
by Judith Head

Judith Head's 1995 novel Culebra Cut *is set in Panama in 1911. The main character,
William Thomas, moves to Culebra, Panama, when his physician father accepts a job in a
local hospital. From his new home, William watches workers construct the Panama Canal.*

William Thomas pushed out the screen and climbed onto the windowsill. Dawn skirted the horizon and coated the sky with faint light. William grinned as he thought how close he was to his dream. Soon he would stand at the edge of Culebra Cut and watch as thousands of workers and machines carved the Panama Canal out of the mountains.

An explosion from the Cut shook the heavy, damp air. William took a breath and jumped down onto the wet grass. The screen slapped against the window frame. He froze, listening for sounds of his parents stirring, but heard nothing.

The world outside was alive with noise. A monkey's howl cracked the air. A bird warbled a melody, and another answered. A soft hum droned near William's ear. He wiped the side of his face and was relieved to find only a thin layer of sweat.

Around his feet the moist air thickened into fog. Careful to keep his eyes on the ground, he headed for the boardwalk behind the house, then quietly followed it among the other dwellings. Where the buildings and boardwalk ended, he stepped off into the thick wet grass.

Another explosion thundered in the Cut. He pictured the dirt and rock being tossed up and tried to run toward it. Matted grass grabbed at his shoes. Wet air filled his lungs. Sweat dripped from his face and tickled his back between his shoulder blades. He hardly noticed.

Where a foot-wide crack split the ground, the grass gave way to mud. William jumped the gap, and slippery, blue-black clay oozed into his shoes. He pulled his feet free and stepped back onto the grass.

Ahead of him the ground disappeared under a dense mist.

"The Cut!" he said excitedly. "It's got to be."

For William being at the site of the largest construction project in history was a miracle. More than a year before, his neighbor, Mr. Fergueson, had served a stint as an engineer on the canal railroad. He had begun sending William issues of the *Canal Record,* the weekly newspaper of the Isthmian Canal Commission, or ICC, and William was hooked. He pored over facts and figures in each issue: the amount of concrete in the canal's six gigantic locks, the number of cubic yards of earth in the breakwater at Colón, the water level of the lake behind Gatun Dam. He pictured the plows scraping fill from trains of flatcars, cheered as Culebra Cut deepened, and grieved at each report of a slide sending dirt and rock tumbling into the Cut. To William an issue of the *Record* was more exciting than an adventure story by Jack London.

During the summer of 1910, when Mr. Fergueson had returned home to Maine, William's father was exhausted and ill. A hard winter traveling on skis or snowshoes tending patients had been followed by a cold, wet spring spent digging his buggy out of the mud. Deep creases lined Dr. Thomas's face, and a cough rumbled in his chest.

"Get away to a warmer place. Panama's the answer," Mr. Fergueson had suggested. "Every one of those villages along the canal has got either a dispensary or a small hospital. . . ."

William was jubilant. "We've just got to go. It'll be as important as watching the Egyptian pyramids being built. You'd want me to see that, wouldn't you?..."

---

dispensary a place where a person can get medicines or first-aid treatment

jubilant joyful

Now, in July 1911, on his first full day in Panama, William stood at the edge of Culebra Cut, the most challenging stretch of the whole canal. He was sure that no place on earth teemed with excitement and purpose like the spot where the Big Ditch was being carved through the mountains. . . .

For hundreds of years people had dream-ed of digging a canal through the narrow Isthmus of Panama. Eliminating the long voyage around South America would make travel between the Atlantic and Pacific Oceans much faster. In 1881, a French company attempted to fulfill that dream. They made plans to dig a canal at sea-level. But almost as soon as work in Culebra Cut had started, wide sections of the bank across from the village of Culebra began sliding toward the bottom. The slides, as well as problems with money and disease, forced the French to give up the project in 1899.

Four years later the United States signed a lease for a ten-mile Canal Zone across the isthmus. The ICC scrapped the idea of a sea-level canal in favor of a lock model, which would allow digging in Culebra Cut to stop at forty feet above sea-level. Even so, the slides were getting worse.

William looked behind him. The houses were only shadows, but a shape like a giant serpent loomed close in the haze. Flatcars! William rushed to the line of train cars standing ready for loads of dirt, then hurried toward the end of the line.

A huge Bucyrus steam shovel, its massive jaws at rest, sat wrapped in fog. Beautiful, he thought, as beautiful as anything nature could produce. And it was powerful too. "Five cubic yards a bite. Ninety-five tons—so big that it takes ten men to run it," he answered to the mist. William knew why the steam shovel was there: to take off the top of the mountain so that it could not slide into the Cut.

A piercing whistle blasted, making William jump. Another joined it. He rushed back to the rim. Beneath the swirling fog, boilers popped, engines bellowed, shovels clanged. Steam merged with mist. The work day had begun.

Gradually the haze lifted to reveal the great gash. Along the opposite side of the Cut, on the sheared cliff that years before had lain deep within the mountain, layers of orange, pink, purple, and red earth blazed in the sun. Here and there, strands of deep green foliage crept down from the hilltops like fingers intent on taking back the land.

Not far below, a steam shovel lay on its side. Surrounding it was a broad wedge of dirt and rock that stretched from the wall to the middle of the Cut's floor. A slide! Just the way Mr. Fergueson had said it would look! William watched eagerly as scores of men scurried about, determining the best way to face this latest setback.

isthmus   a narrow strip of land with water on each side, that joins two larger bodies of land

Think It Over

1. What was the main reason for building the Panama Canal?

2. Could you use this excerpt as a primary source in a report on the Panama Canal? Why or why not?

African Americans During World War I
from *The Journal of Negro History*, edited by Carter G. Woodson
and from *The Big Sea* by Langston Hughes

During World War I, many African Americans moved from the South to northern cities. Often, these newcomers faced discrimination and even violence. At the same time, many African Americans found greater opportunity as a result of the "great migration" to the North. The first selection below is a letter written by a black southerner in response to an advertisement in a northern newspaper. The second is an excerpt from *The Big Sea,* the autobiography of writer Langston Hughes. Hughes moved with his family from Kansas to Cleveland, Ohio. He later became one of the most famous African American poets of the century.

Houston, Tex., 4-29-17

Dear Sir:

I am a constant reader of the "Chicago Defender"* and in your last issue I saw a want ad that appealed to me. I am a Negro, age 37, and am an all round foundry man. . . . [I] hold good references from several shops, in which I have been employed. . . . It is hard for a black man to hold a job here, as prejudice is very strong. I have never been discharged on account of dissatisfaction with my work, but I have been "let out" on account of my color. . . . I have a family and am anxious to leave here, but have not the means, and as wages are not much here, it is very hard to save enough to get away with. If you know of any firms that are in need of a core maker and whom you think would send me transportation, I would be pleased to be put in touch with them . . . If any one will send transportation, I will arrange or agree to have it taken out of my salary until full amount of fare is paid. . . . I am ready to start at any time, and would be pleased to hear something favorable.

Langston Hughes:

I had no sooner graduated from grammar school in Lincoln than we moved from Illinois to Cleveland. My stepfather sent for us. He was working in a steel mill during the war, and making lots of money. But it was hard work, and he never looked the same afterwards. Every day he worked several hours overtime, because they paid well for overtime. But after a while, he couldn't stand the heat of the furnaces, so he got a job as caretaker of a theater building, and after that as janitor of an apartment house.

Rents were very high for colored people in Cleveland, and the Negro district was extremely crowded, because of the great migration. It was difficult to find a place to live. We always lived, during my high school years, either in an attic or a basement, and paid quite a lot for such inconvenient quarters. White people on the east side of the city were moving out of their frame houses and renting them to Negroes at double and triple the rents they could receive from others. An eight-room house with one bath would be cut up into apartments and five or six families crowded into it, each two-room kitchenette apartment renting for what the whole house had rented for before.

But Negroes were coming in in a great tide from the South, and they had to have some place to live. Sheds and garages and store fronts were turned into living quarters. As always, the white neighborhoods resented Negroes moving closer and closer—but when

---

* The *Chicago Defender* was one of the most influential African American newspapers of the time. It often ran articles that urged its readers to come north to find work.

foundry   a place where molten metal is cast in molds

references   statements about one's character and ability

the whites did give way, they gave way at very profitable rentals. So most of the colored people's wages went for rent. The landlords and the banks made it difficult for them to buy houses, so they had to pay the exorbitant rents required. When my stepfather quit the steel mill job, my mother went out to work in service to help him meet expenses. She paid a woman to take care of my little brother while she worked as a maid.

exorbitant not reasonable or not fair

Think It Over

1. How does the man who wrote the letter feel about work? Do you think Langston Hughes's stepfather shared this attitude?

2. How do the two types of primary sources included above differ from one another? Would you consider both of them to be reliable sources of information?

from *A Farewell to Arms*
by Ernest Hemingway

During World War I, Ernest Hemingway worked as an ambulance driver for the Red Cross in Italy. He was 19 years old when he was sent to the front. This excerpt from his novel *A Farewell to Arms* provides a glimpse of what the war was like in Italy. The narrator is a fictional ambulance driver named Frederic Henry. The Italians were fighting against the Austrians, Croatians, and Germans.

The wind rose in the night and at three o'clock in the morning with the rain coming in sheets there was a bombardment and the Croatians came over across the mountain meadows and through patches of woods and into the front line. They fought in the dark in the rain and a counter-attack of scared men from the second line drove them back. There was much shelling and rifle fire all along the line. They did not come again and it was quieter and between the gusts and wind and rain we could hear the sound of a great bombardment far to the north.

The wounded were coming into the post, some were carried on stretchers, some walking and some were brought on the backs of men that came across the field. They were wet to the skin and all were scared. We filled two cars with stretcher cases as they came up from the cellar of the post and as I shut the door of the second car and fastened it I felt the rain on my face turn to snow. The flakes were coming heavy and fast in the rain.

When daylight came the storm was still blowing but the snow had stopped. It had melted as it fell on the wet ground and now it was raining again. There was another attack just after daylight but it was unsuccessful. We expected an attack all day but it did not come until the sun was going down. The bombardment started to the south below the long wooded ridge where the Austrian guns were concentrated. We expected a bombardment but it did not come. It was getting dark. Guns were firing from the field behind the village and the shells, going away, had a comfortable sound.

We heard that the attack to the south had been unsuccessful. They did not attack that night but we heard that they had broken through to the north. In the night word came that we were to prepare to retreat. The captain at the post told me this. He had it from the Brigade. A little while later he came from the telephone and said it was a lie. The Brigade had received orders that the line of the Bainsizza should be held no matter what happened. I asked about the break through and he said that he had heard at the Brigade that the Austrians had broken through the twenty-seventh army corps up toward Caporetto. There had been a great battle in the north all day. . . .

"It's Germans that are attacking," one of the medical officers said. The word Germans was something to be frightened of. We did not want to have anything to do with the Germans. "There are fifteen divisions of Germans," the medical officer said. "They have broken through and we will be cut off."

"At the Brigade, they say this line is to be held. They say they have not broken through badly and that we will hold a line across the mountains from Monte Maggiore."

"Where do they hear this?"

"From the Division."

"The word that we were to retreat came from the Division."

"We work under the Army Corps," I said. "But here I work under you. Naturally when you tell me to go I will go. But get the orders straight."

"The orders are that we stay here. You clear the wounded from here to the clearing station."

bombardment   an attack with bombs or heavy gunfire

concentrated   close together in one place

"Sometimes we clear from the clearing station to the field hospitals too," I said. "Tell me, I have never seen a retreat—if there is a retreat how are all the wounded evacuated?"

"They are not. They take as many as they can and leave the rest."

"What will I take in the cars?"

"Hospital equipment."

"All right," I said.

The next night the retreat started. We heard that Germans and Austrians had broken through in the north and were coming down the mountain valley toward Cividale and Udine. The retreat was orderly, wet, and sullen. In the night, going slowly along the crowded roads we passed troops marching under the rain, guns, horses pulling wagons, mules, motor trucks, all moving away from the front. There was no more disorder than in an advance.

That night we helped empty the field hospitals that had been set up in the least ruined villages of the plateau, taking the wounded down to Plava on the river-bed: and the next day hauled all day in the rain to evacuate the hospital and clearing station at Plava. It rained steadily and the army of the Bainsizza moved down off the plateau in the October rain and across the river where the great victories had commenced in the spring of that year.

sullen   gloomy or dismal

commenced   started or began

Think It Over

1. Why would the ambulances be filled with hospital equipment instead of wounded soldiers during a retreat?

2. *A Farewell to Arms* is a work of fiction. Do you think it could still be a useful source of some information about World War I? Why or why not?

from "I Have a Dream"
by Martin Luther King, Jr.

In August 1963, civil rights groups organized the March on Washington. More than 200,000 people marched to the nation's capital. By their words and massive presence, participants hoped to persuade Congress to pass civil rights laws. On that hot day in August, Martin Luther King, Jr., spoke in front of the Lincoln Memorial. The speech he gave that day became known as the "I Have a Dream" speech. His words moved a nation.

I have a dream that one day, this nation will rise up and live out the true meaning of its creed: "We hold these truths to be self-evident; that all men are created equal. . . ."

I have a dream that my four little children will one day live in a nation where they will not be judged by the color of their skin but by the content of their character.

I have a dream today!

I have a dream that one day the state of Alabama . . . will be transformed into a situation where little black boys and black girls will be able to join hands with little white boys and white girls as sisters and brothers.

I have a dream today!

I have a dream that one day every valley shall be exalted, every hill and mountain shall be made low, the rough places shall be made plain, and the crooked places shall be made straight and the glory of the Lord will be revealed and all flesh shall see it together. This is our hope. This is the faith that I go back to the South with.

With this faith we will be able to hew out of the mountain of despair a stone of hope. With this faith we will be able to transform the jangling discords of our nation into a beautiful symphony of brotherhood.

With this faith we will be able to work together, to pray together, to struggle together, to go to jail together, to stand up for freedom together, knowing that we will be free one day. This will be the day when all of God's children will be able to sing with new meaning—"my country 'tis of thee; sweet land of liberty; of thee I sing; land where my fathers died, land of the pilgrim's pride, from every mountain side, let freedom ring"—and if America is to be a great nation, this must become true.

So let freedom ring from the prodigious hilltops of New Hampshire.

Let freedom ring from the mighty mountains of New York.

Let freedom ring from the heightening Alleghenies of Pennsylvania.

Let freedom ring from the snow-capped Rockies of Colorado.

Let freedom ring from the curvaceous slopes of California.

But not only that.

Let freedom ring from Stone Mountain of Georgia.

Let freedom ring from Lookout Mountain of Tennessee.

Let freedom ring from every hill and molehill of Mississippi. From every mountainside, let freedom ring.

When we let freedom ring, when we let it ring from every village and every hamlet, from every state and every city, we will be able to speed up that day when all of God's children, black men and white men, Jews and Gentiles, Protestants and Catholics, will be able to join hands and sing in the words of the old Negro spiritual: "Free at last! free at last! thank God almighty, we are free at last!"

creed a set of beliefs
exalted raised up
despair loss of hope

discords conflicts
prodigious enormous; huge
curvaceous curving

Think It Over

1. What is the main idea of Martin Luther King, Jr.'s, "I Have a Dream" speech?

2. In his speech, King included quotations from the Declaration of Independence, the Bible, the song "America," and a spiritual. What effect do you think he hoped to have on his audience by including these quotations?

from *Hunger of Memory*
by Richard Rodriguez

Hunger of Memory is about the educational experiences of writer Richard Rodriguez. Rodriguez, the son of Mexican immigrants, grew up in Sacramento, California, during the 1960s. In his book, Rodriguez discusses his problems as a "minority student." In the following selection, Rodriguez discusses how he learned to become a good reader and to appreciate books.

The old nun would read from her favorite books, usually biographies of early American presidents. Playfully she ran through complex sentences, calling the words alive with her voice, making it seem that the author was somehow speaking directly to me.

One day the nun concluded a session by asking me why I was so reluctant to read by myself. I tried to explain; said something about the way written words made me feel all alone—almost, I wanted to add but didn't, as when I spoke to myself in a room just emptied of furniture. She studied my face as I spoke; she seemed to be watching more than listening. In an uneventful voice she replied that I had nothing to fear. Didn't I realize that reading would open up whole new worlds? A book could open doors for me. It could introduce me to people and show me places I never imagined existed. She gestured toward the bookshelves. . . . I listened with respect. I was thinking then of another consequence of literacy, one I was too shy to admit but nonetheless trusted. Books were going to make me 'educated.' That confidence enabled me, several months later, to overcome my fear of the silence.

In fourth grade I embarked upon a grandiose reading program. 'Give me the names of important books,' I would say to startled teachers. They soon found out that I had in mind 'adult books.' I ignored their suggestions of anything written for children. . . . And whatever I read I read for extra credit. Each time I finished a book, I reported the achievement to a teacher and basked in the

praise my effort earned. Despite my best efforts, however, there seemed to be more and more books I needed to read. At the library I would literally tremble as I came upon whole shelves of books I hadn't read. So I read and I read and I read: *Great Expectations;* all the short stories of Kipling; *The Babe Ruth Story;* the entire first volume of the *Encyclopedia Britannica* (A-ANSTEY); the *Iliad; Moby Dick; Gone With the Wind; The Good Earth; Ramona; Forever Amber; The Lives of the Saints; Crime and Punishment; The Pearl.* . . . Librarians who initially frowned when I checked out the maximum ten books at a time started saving books they thought I might like. Teachers would say to the rest of the class. "I only wish the rest of you took reading as seriously as Richard obviously does.' . . .

What did I see in my books? I had the idea that they were crucial for my academic success, though I couldn't have said exactly how or why. In the sixth grade I simply concluded that what gave a book its value was some major idea or theme it contained. If that core essence could be mined and memorized, I would become learned like my teachers. I decided to record in a notebook the themes of the books that I read. After reading *Robinson Crusoe*, I wrote that its theme was 'the value of learning to live by oneself.' When I completed *Wuthering Heights*, I noted the danger of 'letting emotions get out of control.' Rereading these brief moralistic appraisals usually left me disheartened. I couldn't believe that they were really the

reluctant unwilling
consequence result or outcome
literacy the ability to read and write
embarked started or began
grandiose impressive

basked enjoyed a pleasant feeling
crucial of the greatest importance; critical
moralistic appraisals judgments about the rightness or wrongness
disheartened discouraged

source of reading's value. But for many more years, they constituted the only means I had of describing to myself the educational value of books.

In spite of my earnestness, I found reading a pleasurable activity. I came to enjoy the lonely good company of books. Early on weekday mornings, I'd read in my bed. I'd feel a mysterious comfort then, reading in the dawn quiet—the blue-gray silence interrupted by the occasional churning of the refrigerator motor a few rooms away or the more distant sounds of a city bus beginning its run. On weekends I'd go to the public library to read, surrounded by old men and women. Or, if the weather was fine, I would take my books to the park and read in the shade of a tree. A warm summer evening was my favorite reading time. Neighbors would leave for vacation and I would water their lawns. I would sit through the twilight on the front porches or in backyards, reading to the cool, whirling sounds of sprinklers. . . .

There were pleasures to sustain me after I'd finish my books. Carrying a volume back to the library, I would be pleased by its weight. I'd run my fingers along the edge of the pages and marvel at the breadth of my achievement. Around my room, growing stacks of paperback books reinforced my assurance.

I entered high school having read hundreds of books. My habit of reading made me a confident speaker and writer of English. Reading also enabled me to sense something of the shape, the major concerns, of Western thought. (I was able to say something about Dante and Descartes and Engels and James Baldwin in my high school term papers.) In these various ways, books brought me academic success as I hoped that they would.

constituted   formed; composed

earnestness   seriousness

Think It Over

1. In the above passage, Richard Rodriguez is retelling his own childhood experiences. Do you think his words could be used to support any particular cause? Explain.

The Volunteer Spirit: Three Views
from *Who Cares? Millions Do: A Book About Altruism* by Milton Meltzer

Many young people decide to volunteer their time and talent by spending several years as members of the Peace Corps. The Peace Corps program, started in 1961 by President John Kennedy, gives young people the opportunity to live in another culture and teach skills to others. The first two passages below are from Peace Corps volunteers in the Philippines and in Paraguay. In the third account, a fish farmer in Thailand tells how the Peace Corps volunteers helped him.

Dennis Drake:

My first introduction to the [Peace] Corps was via a television advertisement that ran under the slogan, "The toughest job you'll ever love." Perhaps it was partly the slogan that got me thinking about joining or just the chance to change my life and help people at the same time. Really a simplistic view but maybe common thinking for more than just a few volunteers. Just imagine a person thinking he can actually do something about world hunger, poverty, illiteracy, or disease. Those are not "just" problems, but problems the size of mountains, yet the average Peace Corps volunteer believes he can do his part by chipping away at those mountains . . . one person at a time.

Kathleen Maria Sloop:

At the time I received my assignment from Washington, I had just been promoted to a great position as a market analyst in the bank at which I was working. I was a recent college graduate, so it was hard to give up all the things I had recently acquired, like a car, a good job, a nice house that I was sharing with two roommates whom I loved. But, I also knew that I'd learn more as a PCV [Peace Corps volunteer], and I'd be "richer" as a person, if I lived and ate and shared with people who needed my help and friendship. I saw I was easily slipping into the easy, yet sometimes empty, materialistic life

we Americans lead. I wanted to do something that would remind me for the rest of my life that Americans' lifestyles are atypical, not the norm in the world. It was hard to give up the convenience and comfort of the U.S., and I won't say there haven't been times when I wished I could blink and be home again, but I've also never regretted making the decision I did to serve.

Mr. Prakong:

Volunteers have helped me a lot in two different ways: first, with their labor, helping me to run the farm—just proving that they are willing to "get their feet wet" alongside me. They dress in jeans, they put on "farmer pants," sometimes they get diseases or infections, but that's the way they work. The other way they help is that volunteers know something about how to raise fish, the different species, what [food] they need. I never knew anything like that before volunteers came. They taught me induced fish spawning techniques, they helped me build signs on the road to market my fish. . . . Before the volunteers came, I was a "blind man" in terms of fish breeding. . . . If I had to rely on government administrations, I would be starving by now. They work from the top down, they are eager to show off their technical expertise, but they don't know the faces of the people they want to instruct. Peace Corps volunteers work from the bottom up.

illiteracy   the condition of not being able to read or write
materialistic   being more concerned with material things than with spiritual values

atypical   not normal

They have the theory, but they are not afraid to get their feet wet, to work one-on-one with the farmers.

Working this way with Volunteers, a very close relationship develops. I am the "older brother," the Volunteer is the "younger brother or sister." We suffer the same problems together, we sit together, we eat together—sometimes don't eat together if there's no food—joke together. We are family. I cried when the last Volunteer left. I will cry when Ron Rice (my Volunteer coworker) leaves.

Think It Over

1. Author Milton Meltzer collected these three accounts for a book titled *Who Cares? Millions Do: A Book About Altruism.* (Altruism means unselfish concern for others.) Do you think Meltzer wanted to present a positive view of the Peace Corps? How might this have influenced what he included in his book?

Literature
★★★★★

MEXICO
"The Talking Stone"
from *The Hungry Woman: Myths and Legends of the Aztecs*, edited by John Bierhorst

The Aztec empire was at its greatest under the rule of Montezuma in the early 1500's. Still, there were signs that the end of the empire might be near. One of these signs was described in the legend of the talking stone.

Montezuma loved nothing more than to order great monuments that would make him famous. Beautiful things, it was true, had been commissioned by the kings who had gone before, but to Montezuma those works were insignificant. "Not splendid enough for Mexico," he would say, and as the years went by he grew to have doubts about even the huge round-stone where prisoners were sacrificed to Huitzilopochtli. "I want a new one," he said at last, "and I want it a forearm wide and two forearms taller."

So the order went out to the stonecutters to search the countryside for a boulder that could be carved into a round-stone a forearm wider and two forearms taller. When the proper stone had been sighted, at a place called Acolco, haulers and lifters were summoned from six cities and told to bring ropes and levers. Using their levers, they pried the stone from the hillside and dragged it to a level spot to be carved. As soon as it was in position, thirty stonecutters began to chisel it with their flint chisels, making it not only bigger than any round-stone that had been seen before, but more unusual and more beautiful. During the time that they worked, they ate only the rarest delicacies, sent by Montezuma and served by the people of Acolco.

When the stone was ready to be taken to Mexico, the carvers sent word to the king, who ordered the temple priests to go bring incense and a supply of quails. Arriving at the stone, the priests decorated it with paper streamers, perfumed it with the incense, and spattered molten rubber. Then they twisted

the necks of the quails and spattered quail blood. There were musicians, too, with conch horns and skin drums. And comedians also came, so that the stone could be entertained as it traveled along.

But when they tried to pull it, it would not be moved. It seemed to have grown roots, and all the ropes snapped as if they had been cotton threads. Two more cities were ordered to send haulers, and as they set to work, shouting back and forth, trussing it with fresh ropes, the stone spoke up and said, "Try what you will."

Suddenly the shouting stopped. "Why do you pull me?" said the stone. "I am not about to turn over and go, I am not to be pulled where you want me to go."

Quietly the men kept working. "Then pull me," it said. "I'll talk to you later." And with that the stone slid forward, traveling easily as far as Tlapitzahuayan. There the haulers decided to rest for the day, while two stone-cutters went ahead to warn Montezuma that the great stone had begun to talk.

"Are you drunk?" said the king when they gave him the news. "Why come here telling me lies?" Then he called for his storekeeper and had the two messengers locked up. But he sent six lords to find out the truth, and when they had heard the stone say, "Try what you will, I am not to be pulled," they went back to Mexico and reported it to Montezuma, and the two prisoners were set free.

In the morning the stone spoke again. "Will you never understand? Why do you pull me? I am not to be taken to Mexico. Tell Montezuma it is no use. The time is

Huitzilopochtli   war-like Mexican god who guided Aztecs to found their empire
delicacies   special foods, especially those hard to find or prepare

incense   perfume made to be burned, often used in religious ceremonies
molten   melted

bad, and his end is near. He has tried to make himself greater than our lord who created the sky and the earth. But pull me if you must, you poor ones. Let's go." And with that the stone slid along until it reached Itztapalapan.

Again it halted, and again they sent messengers to tell Montezuma what it had said. Just as before, he flew into a rage, but this time he was secretly frightened, and although he refused to give the messengers credit for bringing him the truth, he stopped short of jailing them and told them to go back and carry out his orders.

The next morning, as the haulers picked up their ropes, they found that the stone once again moved easily, sliding as far as the causeway that led to Mexico. Advised that the stone had reached the other side of the water, Montezuma sent priests to greet it with flowers and incense, also to appease it with blood sacrifices in case it might be angry. Again it started to move. But when it was halfway across the lake, it stopped and said, "Here and no farther," and although the causeway was made of cedar beams seven hands thick, the stone broke through them, crashing into the water with a noise like thunder. All the men who were tied to

the ropes were dragged down and killed, and many others were wounded.

Told what had happened, Montezuma himself came onto the causeway to see where the stone had disappeared. Still thinking he would carry out his plan, he ordered divers to search the bottom of the lake to see if the stone had settled in a place where it might be hauled back to dry land. But they could find neither the stone itself nor any sign of the men who had been killed. The divers were sent down a second time, and when they came back up they said, "Lord, we see a narrow trace in the water leading toward Acolco."

"Very well," said Montezuma, and with no further questioning he sent his stonecutters back to Acolco to see what they might discover, and when they returned, they reported no more than what the king already knew. Still tied with its ropes and spattered with incense and blood offerings, the stone had gone back to the hillside where it had originally been found.

Then Montezuma turned to his lords and said, "Brothers, I know now that our pains and troubles will be many and our days will be few. As for me, just as with the kings that have gone before, I must let myself die. May the Lord of Creation do what he pleases."

causeway   a land bridge connecting two bodies of land separated by water

Think It Over

1. Why did Montezuma insist on moving the stone? How did his feelings change as the story progressed?

2. What message did this legend give to the Aztecs? What message about the environment could it have for people today?

Eyewitness Account ★★★★★

GEOGRAPHY

MEXICO

We Live in Mexico
by Valentin Lugo

Valentin Lugo, a train engineer on the Chihuahua-Pacific line, loves his country's many different lands. He describes some of the scenery on his route, crossing northern Mexico from Ojinaga in the northeast to Topolobampo on the Pacific coast.

Traveling on the Chihuahua-Pacific line is a real adventure. It starts in Ojinaga, a town on the border with the U.S., in the State of Chihuahua. From Ojinaga I drive the train across Chihuahua's hot, semi-arid plains to the state capital itself, Chihuahua. This part of the journey is mainly through cattle-raising country, but after Chihuahua city, the train starts its climb into the forests of the Sierra Madre Occidental, a range of mountains which runs down Mexico parallel to the Pacific coast.

The mountain scenery which I see from my cab is quite breathtaking, particularly when the train passes through an area called the Tarahumaran Sierra, named after the Tarahumaran Indians who live there. This small part of Mexico has been designated an area of outstanding scenery, with deep canyons cut into the rocks by mountain torrents.

While in the mountains, the train constantly climbs and drops, through splendid scenery, twisting in all directions over thirty-nine bridges and through eighty tunnels, sometimes crossing above or below its own railroad tracks. At one point, the train reaches an altitude of nearly 2,438 meters (8,000 feet)!

All too soon, the train descends from the mountains to the low-lying land of the coast to meet the Gulf of California and Pacific Ocean at the port of Topolobampo in the State of Sinaloa. In all, the journey is 920 km (572 miles) and takes almost a day to complete.

I have been driving this train ever since the line opened in 1961. The route took nearly a century to plan and build, and runs through some of the last great places of mountain wilderness in Mexico. The engineers who built the line moved an estimated 14.5 million cubic meters (19 million cubic yards) of earth!

Nearly all the passengers who travel on my train are sightseers. But there are other trains running on the line which carry such cargoes as cotton, timber, cattle, gold, silver, copper, zinc, and manganese. At some points along the line, the trains can only travel at 10 kph (6 mph) because of the steepness of the grade.

Mexico has an extensive rail system, with over 32,000 km (19,900 miles) of track. The railroads were completely nationalized in 1970, and are now run by the National Mexican Railways. Most trains have a first- and second-class section and sleepers can be reserved for overnight journeys. Most Mexicans travel in the second-class section. American tourists, in particular, like to travel first class, which has pullman type seats and a restaurant car. Yes, Mexico has a lot to offer to the tourists, and what better way to see it than from the window of a train?

semi-arid   very dry, but not as dry as a true desert
torrents   fast flowing waters

pullman   a kind of seat that is very comfortable

MEXICO

We Live in Mexico
by Fernando Hernandez

As Mexico's population grows, scientists like Fernando Hernandez know that new sources of food must be found. Fernando thinks the seas around Mexico can be one of those sources, but only if the wildlife can be protected. Fernando is helping do that with a project that studies and conserves the marine turtles that live and nest on Mexico's shores.

Mexico has over 9,368 km (5,821 miles) of coastline facing seas which have some of the richest fishing zones in the world. The east coast faces the Gulf of Mexico and the Caribbean Sea. There, fishermen catch red snapper, snook, bass, kingfish, pompano, mullet and shrimp. The west coast faces the Pacific Ocean and from there come lobster, tuna, shrimp, and sardine.

The Mexican fishing industry has greatly expanded in recent years, growing from a catch of about 390,000 tons ten years ago, to a catch of about 800,000 tons today. Up to now, fish hasn't been consumed in large quantities in Mexico—vegetables such as corn and beans have been the basic ingredients of meals here for thousands of years. But I believe that Mexico is now over-populated and that in the near future will rely more and more on the sea for its food. The government is slowly becoming aware of this, and now money is being invested in projects researching both the effects of pollution and the study of marine life, particularly endangered species of fish and other marine animals.

My work as a marine biologist concentrates on the marine turtle. This animal is common in tropical waters the world over, and of the eight species that are known to

exist, seven can be found in the waters off both the east and west coasts of Mexico.

Six months of my year are spent on the beaches of various states such as Sinaloa, Colima, Michoacán, Guerrero, Oaxaca and Tamaulipas, where the turtles come ashore to lay their eggs and then return to the sea. Part of my job is to tag a turtle while it is on the beach. The tag is fixed to the turtle's fin, and carries such data as the date and the country and beach of tagging. That way if the turtle is found again, perhaps by a marine biologist in another country, we can estimate how far the creature swims. I once received a tag taken from a turtle that had been caught off the French coast at Biarritz, the other side of the Atlantic Ocean!

I also protect the eggs from dogs, coyotes, racoons and even pigs. Unfortunately, many people in Mexico, and in other Latin American countries, consider turtle eggs as a delicacy and take them to sell. The Mexican government has outlawed this practice, but it still goes on despite efforts to prevent it.

I feel the world should be more conscious of the marine environment and do more to help conserve the turtle, and other endangered species like the whale, before they disappear altogether.

endangered species   kinds of plants or animals that are in danger of becoming extinct, or dying out completely

BRAZIL

from *Rain Forest Amerindians*
the words of Ailton Drenak
by Anna Lewington

Ailton Krenak is an activist working to protect the rain forests of Brazil from development. A member of the Krenak people, Ailton wants to preserve the way of life of the many Amerindian groups living in the rain forest.

We have lived in this place for a long time, a very long time, since the time when the world did not yet have this shape. We learned with the ancients that we are a tiny part of this immense universe, fellow travelers with all the animals, the plants, and the waters. We are all a part of the whole. We cannot neglect or destroy our home. And now we want to talk to those who cannot yet manage to see the world in this way, to say to them that together we have to take care of the boat in which we are all sailing.

Think It Over

1. What might be some good and bad effects on the land of building a train route like the one Valentin Lugo travels? How might Ailton Krenak feel about such a train route if it went through his people's land?

2. Why is it so important for the people of Mexico to preserve marine life such as the turtle? Why might it be difficult for some people to follow the laws protecting the marine turtles?

3. How do all three of these men feel about the land in which they live? Explain your answers.

　　　　　　　　　　　　　　　　Readings From Social Studies　**87**

PANAMA

"The Story of the Panama Canal"
by Nancy Winslow Parker

Imagine trying to cut a river across a continent! That dream took nearly 500 years to complete.

For at least 400 years people dreamed about digging a canal across the Isthmus of Panama, a skinny strip of mosquito-infested jungle measuring 37 miles wide by 480 miles long in Central America. It is the narrowest strip of land in the Western Hemisphere. For ships sailing from New York to San Francisco, or the other way around, the canal would cut 7,800 miles. It would eliminate the long and dangerous sea journey around South America and Cape Horn, the terror of seamen. A canal would save weeks, if not months, of travel.

But none of the dreamers could foresee the horrible suffering, disease, death, and failures that would befall those who tried to change Panama's Chagres, the "River of Crocodiles," into a canal that would carry ships from ocean to ocean.

The first dreamer was King Charles V of Spain. In 1534 his soldiers had to struggle across the Isthmus on a bumpy stone road, El Camino Real, with the stolen riches of Bolivia and Peru piled on the backs of mules and horses. The road went from Panama City on the Pacific to Nombre de Dios and later Portobelo on the Caribbean, where the gold and silver were loaded onto ships and carried across the sea to Spain.

About 300 years later, in 1849, gold was discovered in California. Fortune seekers swarmed across the Isthmus by mule, by canoe, and on foot to Panama City, where they could board sailing ships for San Francisco. By 1855, despite many deaths from malaria and yellow fever, an American company succeeded in completing a railroad across the Isthmus to transport the prospectors and their families.

In 1882 the French began digging a great trench—*la Grande Tranchée*—across the Isthmus. It had been the dream of Ferdinand de Lesseps, but his canal company ultimately collapsed because of disease, corruption, and mismanagement. In 1889 the French abandoned the partially excavated canal, leaving costly dredges, steam shovels, derricks, and buildings to be swallowed up by the Panamanian jungle.

James Stanley Gilbert's poems are about life on the Isthmus. He lived there during the French effort to build a canal and the first years of the American canal-building effort. His poem "Beyond the Chagres" documents some of the horrors the workers faced every day in what was at that time one of the worst pestholes on earth. Gilbert had seen the workers stricken with malaria, yellow fever, bubonic plague, and alcoholism, and watched the daily trains carrying bodies to the cemetery on nearby Monkey Hill.

Americans came to Panama in 1904 to take up the challenge of building a canal. They were well aware of the problems on the Isthmus, and they made two important decisions. The first was to get rid of the mosquitoes in order to reduce disease. The second was to build a lock-and-lake canal, not a sea-level canal as the French had tried to do. There was just too much water on the Isth-

---

isthmus   a narrow strip of land connecting two larger areas of land
foresee   predict
malaria and yellow fever   diseases common in the jungle
corruption   dishonesty
mismanagement   bad planning

excavated   dug
dredges, derricks   construction equipment
pestholes   place full of pests or problems, such as bugs and disease
lock-and-lake canal   a canal in which several lakes at different elevations are connected by a series of locks

mus for a sea-level canal. With a lock-and-lake canal, the flooding of the Chagres River during the rainy season and the drainage of the water along the Isthmus could be controlled by a dam, and the tidal variations of the Pacific Ocean could be accommodated.

It took the Americans ten years of hard work and the involvement of diplomats, engineers, scientists, steel and cement manufacturers, and thousands of pick-and-shovel workers before the dream could be realized. In 1914 the Panama Canal was opened to ships from any country in the world.

tidal variations   because the canal is so close to the Pacific Ocean, its water level rises and falls as the ocean's tides change

diplomats   government workers whose job is to work out problems between their government and the governments of other countries

Name _____   Date _____

Literature
★★★★★

PANAMA

"Beyond the Chagres"
by James Stanley Gilbert

Controlling nature has inspired people to extreme efforts since the beginning of time. For
James Stanley Gilbert, the Panama Canal was that great effort. He was fascinated by the
Canal and the task of taming the Panamanian jungle. Gilbert wrote many poems about the
building of the canal and about his experiences in Panama.

Beyond the Chagres River
   Are paths that lead to death—
To the fever's deadly breezes,
   To malaria's poisonous breath!
Beyond the tropic foliage,
   Where the alligator waits,
Are the mansions of the Devil—
   His original estates!

Beyond the Chagres River
   Are paths fore'er unknown,
With a spider 'neath each pebble,
   A scorpion 'neath each stone.
'Tis here the boa-constrictor
   His fatal banquet holds,
And to his slimy bosom
   His hapless guest enfolds!

Beyond the Chagres River
   Lurks the cougar in his lair,
And ten hundred thousand dangers
   Hide in the noxious air.
Behind the trembling leaflets
   Beneath the fallen reeds,
Are ever-present perils
   Of a million different breeds!

Beyond the Chagres River
   'Tis said—the story's old—
Are paths that lead to mountains
   Of purest virgin gold!
But 'tis my firm conviction
   Whatever tales they tell,
That beyond the Chagres River
   All paths lead straight to hell!

tropic foliage   plants common to tropical lands
fore'er   forever
'neath   beneath
'tis   It is
banquet   large meal

hapless   unsuspecting
enfolds   wraps around
lair   home and hiding place
noxious   poisonous
leaflets   small leaves

Think It Over

1. How did James Stanley Gilbert feel about the Panamanian jungle?
How do you think the people who live in the jungle feel about it? What
might explain the differences in the two sets of feelings?

2. What might be some effects of the Panama Canal for those using it
and for those living where it was built? How do you think the Canal
changed the land itself?

CHILE
"A Huge Black Umbrella"
by Marjorie Agosin

Every now and then a special person enters our lives—someone we always remember. Perhaps that person teaches us an important lesson or maybe just helps us through a difficult time. For the narrator of this story, Delfina Nahuenhual was that special person.

When she arrived at our house she was covered by a huge black umbrella. A white gardenia hung from her left ear. My sister Cynthia and I were **bewitched** by the sight of her.

We were a little afraid, too. She seemed like an enormous fish or a shipwrecked lady far from home. Certainly, her umbrella was useless in the rain since it was ripped in many places, which let the rainwater fall on her—water from one of the few downpours of that surprisingly dry summer. It was the summer in which my sister and I understood why magical things happen, such as the arrival of Delfina Nahuenhual.

My mother welcomed her, and Delfina, with a certain boldness, explained that she always traveled accompanied by that enormous umbrella, which protected her from the sun, elves, and little girls like us. My mother's delicate lips smiled. From that moment my mother and Delfina developed a much friendlier relationship than is usual between "the lady of the house" and "her servant."

Delfina Nahuenhual—we had to call her by her full name—was one of the few survivors of the Chillán earthquake in the south of Chile. She had lost her children, house, her wedding gown, chickens, and two of her favorite lemon trees. All she could rescue was that huge black umbrella covered with dust and forgotten things.

In the evening she usually lit a small stove for cooking; the fire gave off a very lovely, sweet light. Then she wrapped herself up in an enormous shawl of blue wool that wasn't scratchy and she put a few slices of potato on her temples to protect herself from sickness and cold drafts.

As we sat by the stove, Delfina Nahuenhual told stories about tormented souls and frogs that became princes. Her generous lap rocked us back and forth, and her voice made us sleepy. We were peaceful children who felt the healing power of her love. After she thought we were asleep, Delfina Nahuenhual would write long letters that she would later number and wrap up in newspaper. She kept the letters in an old pot that was filled with garlic, cumin, and slivers of lemon rind.

My sister and I always wanted to read those letters and learn the name and address of the person who would receive them. So whenever Delfina Nahuenhual was busy in the kitchen, we tried peeking into the pot to discover what she was hiding.

But we never managed to read the letters. Delfina Nahuenhual would smile at us and shoo us along with the end of her broom.

For many years, Delfina continued to tell us stories next to the stove. Not long after my brother Mario, the spoiled one of the family, was born, Delfina Nahuenhual told us that she was tired and that she wanted to return to the south of Chile. She said she now had some savings and a chicken, which was enough to live on. I thought that she wanted to die and go to heaven because she had decided to return to the mosses and clays of her land.

I remember that I cried a lot when we said good-bye. My brother Mario clung to her full skirt, not wanting to be separated from the wise woman who, for us, was never a servant. When she bent over to give me a kiss, she said that I must give her letters to the person to whom she had addressed them but that I could keep the pot.

bewitched   fascinated

cumin   a spice

For many years, I kept her little pot like a precious secret, a kind of magical lamp in which my childhood was captured. When I wanted to remember her, I rubbed the pot, I smelled it, and all my fears, including my fear of darkness, vanished. After she left I began to understand that my childhood had gone with her. Now more than ever I miss the dish of lentils that she prepared for good luck and prosperity on New Year's Eve. I miss the smell of her skin and her magical stories.

Many years later, my sister Cynthia had her first daughter. Mario went traveling abroad and I decided to spend my honeymoon on Easter Island, that remote island in the middle of the Pacific Ocean, six hours by plane from Chile. It is a place full of mysterious, gigantic statues called Moais. Ever since I was a child, I had been fascinated by those eerie statues, their enormous figures seeming to spring from the earth, just as Delfina Nahuenhual and her huge black umbrella did when she first came to my house. I carried her letters, which I had long ago taken from the small earthen pot and placed in a large moss-green chest along with the few cloves of garlic that still remained. As a grown-up I never had the urge to read the letters. I only knew that they should be delivered to someone.

eerie strange, mysterious
leper colony Leprosy is a skin disease which was once very contagious. Lepers were kept in closed communities to prevent the disease from spreading.

One morning when the sun shone even in the darkest corner of my hotel room, I went to the address written on Delfina's letters. It was a leper colony, one of the few that still exist. A very somber employee opened the door and quickly took the packet of five hundred letters from me. I asked if the addressee was still alive and he said of course, but that I couldn't meet the person. When I gave him the letters, it seemed as though I had lost one of my most valuable possessions, perhaps even the last memories of my dear Delfina Nahuenhual's life.

So I never did meet the person to whom Delfina Nahuenhual wrote her letters nor learned why she spent her sleepless nights writing them. I only learned that he was a leper on Easter Island, that he was still alive and, perhaps, still reads the letters, the dreams of love Delfina Nahuenhual had each night. When I returned home, I knew at last that Delfina Nahuenhual was content, because when I looked up, as she had taught me to do, I saw a huge black umbrella hovering in the cloudy sky.

Chile has suffered many disasters, some natural and some political, and Chileans have had to do their best to rebuild their lives wherever they have relocated.

somber serious

Think It Over

1. Why did Delfina carry her black umbrella everywhere? What did it mean to her?

2. How did Delfina's pot help the narrator feel safe?

FALKLAND ISLANDS

"Whose Falkland Islands Are They?"
by Prime Minister Margaret Thatcher

The Falkland Islands are in the South Atlantic Ocean, off the coast of southern Argentina. They have been under British colonial rule since the 1830's, although Argentina also claimed the islands. In 1982, Argentina took the islands by force. The British sent troops to take the islands back. Some in Great Britain questioned this decision to use force. In this speech, British Prime Minister Margaret Thatcher justified her actions.

In a series of measured and progressive steps, over the past weeks, our forces have tightened their grip of the Falkland Islands. They have retaken South Georgia. Gradually they have denied fresh supplies to the Argentine garrison.

Finally, by the successful amphibious landing at San Carlos Bay in the early hours of Friday morning, they have placed themselves in a position to retake the islands and reverse the illegal Argentine invasion.

By the skill of our pilots, our sailors, and those manning the Rapier missile batteries onshore, they have inflicted heavy losses on the Argentine air force—over fifty fixed-wing aircraft have been destroyed.

There have, of course, been tragic losses. You will have heard of the further attacks on our task force. HMS *Coventry* came under repeated air attack yesterday evening and later sank. One of our merchant marine ships, the *Atlantic Conveyor*, supporting the task force, was also damaged and had to be abandoned. We do not yet know the number of casualties, but our hearts go out to all those who had men in these ships.

Despite these grievous losses, our resolve is not weakened. . . .

It was eight weeks ago today that information reached us that the Argentine fleet was sailing towards the Falklands.

Eight thousand miles away. . . .

And so, seven weeks to the day after the invasion, we moved to recover by force what was taken from us by force. It cannot be said too often: we are the victims; they are the aggressors.

As always, we came to military action reluctantly.

But when territory which has been British for almost 150 years is seized and occupied; when not only British land but British citizens are in the power of an aggressor—then we have to restore our rights and the rights of the Falkland Islanders.

There have been a handful of questioning voices raised here at home. I would like to answer them. It has been suggested that the size of the Falkland Islands and the comparatively small number of its inhabitants—some eighteen hundred men, women, and children—should somehow affect our reaction to what has happened to them.

To those—not many—who speak lightly of a few islanders beyond the seas and who ask the question "Are they worth fighting for?" let me say this: right and wrong are not measured by a head count of those to whom that wrong has been done. That would not be principle but expediency.

And the Falklanders, remember, are not strangers. They are our own people. As the prime minister of New Zealand, Bob Muldoon, put it in his usual straightforward way, "With the Falkland Islanders, it is family."

When their land was invaded and their homes were overrun, they naturally turned to us for help, and we, their fellow citizens, eight thousand miles away in our much larger island, could not and did not beg to be excused.

measured   thought out carefully
garrison   army camp
amphibious   vehicles that can travel on land or water

manning   running, operating
grievous   sad, causing grief

We sent our men and our ships with all speed, hoping against hope that we would not have to use them in battle but prepared to do so if all attempts at a peaceful solution failed. When those attempts failed, we could not sail by on the other side.

And let me add this. If we, the British, were to shrug our shoulders at what has happened in the South Atlantic and acquiesce in the illegal seizure of those faraway islands, it would be a clear signal to those with similar designs on the territory of others to follow in the footsteps of aggression.

Surely we, of all people, have learned the lesson of history: that to appease an aggressor is to invite aggression elsewhere, and on an ever-increasing scale.

Other voices—again only a few—have accused us of clinging to colonialism or even imperialism. Let me remind those who advance that argument that the British have a record second to none of leading colony after colony to freedom and independence. We cling not to colonialism but self-determination.

Still others—again only a few—say we must not put at risk our investments and interests in Latin America; that trade and commerce are too important to us to put in jeopardy some of the valuable markets of the world.

But what would the islanders, under the heel of the invader, say to that?

What kind of people would we be if, enjoying the birthright of freedom ourselves, we abandoned British citizens for the sake of commercial gain?

Now we are present in strength on the Falkland Islands.

Our purpose is to repossess them. We shall carry on until that purpose is accomplished.

When the invader has left, there will be much to do—rebuilding, restoring homes and farms, and, above all, renewing the confidence of the people in their future.

Their wishes will need time to crystallize and, of course, will depend in some measure on what we and others are prepared to do to develop the untapped resources and safeguard the islands' future.

Madam Chairman, our cause is just.

It is the cause of freedom and the rule of law.

It is the cause of support for the weak against aggression by the strong.

Let us, then, draw together in the name, not of jingoism, but of justice.

And let our nation, as it has so often in the past, remind itself—and the world:

Nought shall make us rue,
If England to herself do rest but true.

acquiesce agree to, allow to happen
seizure taking
appease try to keep happy
colonialism/imperialism the rule of one country over another that is far away
repossess own or have again
crystallize become firm and clear

untapped not yet used
jingoism Thatcher is saying that she's not fighting for the Falklands just because she believes they belong to Great Britain but because she believes they have been taken unjustly.
nought nothing
rue regret

Think It Over

1. What reasons did Margaret Thatcher give to justify her actions in sending troops to the Falkland Islands?

2. How did physical geography affect Great Britain's attempt to protect the land and people of the Falkland Islands?

FRENCH CANADA

from *Shadows on the Rock*

by Willa Cather

The city of Quebec sits on a cliff near the St. Lawrence River in southeastern Canada. The city has two parts, an Upper Town which is at the top of the cliff and a Lower Town at the river's edge. In the late 1600's, the city was a colony of France. Each summer boats brought news and supplies from France. Once winter began, the boats could no longer make the crossing. The colony was isolated from France until the next year. In this story, young Cécile cares for her father, Auclair, who is the town pharmacist.

It was late in the afternoon when Auclair left the Château and made his way through the garden of the Récollet friars, past the new Bishop's Palace, and down to his own house. He lived on the steep, winding street called Mountain Hill, which was the one and only thoroughfare connecting the Upper Town with the Lower. The Lower Town clustered on the strip of beach at the foot of the cliff, the Upper Town crowned its summit. Down the face of the cliff there was but this one path, which had probably been a mere watercourse when Champlain and his men first climbed up it to plant the French lilies on the crest of the naked rock. The watercourse was now a steep, stony street, with shops on one side and the retaining walls of the Bishop's Palace on the other. Auclair lived there for two reasons: to be close at hand where Count Frontenac could summon him quickly to the Château, and because, thus situ-ated on the winding stairway connecting the two halves of Quebec, his services were equally accessible to the citizens of both.

On entering his door the apothecary found the front shop empty, lit by a single candle. In the living-room behind, which was partly shut off from the shop by a partition made of shelves and cabinets, a fire burned in the fireplace, and the round din-ing-table was already set with a white cloth, silver candlesticks, glasses, and two clear decanters, one of red wine and one of white.

Behind the living-room there was a small, low-roofed kitchen, built of stone, though the house itself was built of wood in the earliest Quebec manner,—double walls, with saw-dust and ashes filling in the space between the two frames, making a protection nearly four feet thick against the winter cold. From this stone kitchen at the back two pleasant emanations greeted the chemist: the rich odour of roasting fowl, and a child's voice, singing. When he closed the heavy wooden door behind him, the voice called: "Is it you, Papa?"

His daughter ran in from the kitchen,—a little girl of twelve, beginning to grow tall, wearing a short skirt and a sailor's jersey, with her brown hair shingled like a boy's.

Auclair stooped to kiss her flushed cheek. *"Pas de clients?"* he asked.

"Mais, oui! Beaucoup de clients. But they all wanted very simple things. I found them quite easily and made notes of them. But why were you gone so long? Is Monsieur le Comte ill?"

"Not ill, exactly, but there is troublesome news from Montreal."

"Please change your coat now, Papa, and light the candles. I am so anxious about the poulet. . . . The daughter's eyes were shaped like her father's, but were much darker, a

château   castle
thoroughfare   road or path that runs through
clustered   gathered in a group
mere   only, just
apothecary   pharmacist
decanter   pitcher
emanations   sounds and smells coming out from

odour   odor, smell
shingled   layered
Pas de clients?   Didn't any clients come?
Mais, oui! Beaucoup de clients.   My, yes! Many
   clients came.
Monsieur le Comte   Mister, the Count
poulet   chicken

very dark blue, almost black when she was excited, as she was now about the roast. Her mother had died two years ago, and she made the ménage for her father.

Contrary to the custom of his neighbours, Auclair dined at six o'clock in winter and seven in summer, after the day's work was over, as he was used to do in Paris,—though even there almost everyone dined at midday. He now dropped the curtains over his two shop windows, a sign to his neighbours that he was not to be disturbed unless for serious reasons. Having put on his indoor coat, he lit the candles and carried in the heavy soup tureen for his daughter.

They ate their soup in appreciative silence, both were a little tired. . . .

"Papa," she said as he began to carve, "what is the earliest possible time that Aunt Clothilde and Aunt Blanche can get our letters?"

Auclair deliberated. Every fall the colonists asked the same question of one another and reckoned it all anew. "Well, if *La Bonne Espérance* has good luck, she can make La Rochelle in six weeks. Of course, it has been done in five. But let us say six; then, if the roads are bad, and they are likely to be in December, we must count on a week to Paris."

"And if she does not have good luck?"

"Ah, then who can say? But unless she meets with very heavy storms, she can do it in two months. With this west wind, which we can always count on, she will get out of the river and through the Gulf very speedily, and that is sometimes the most tedious part of the voyage. When we came over with the Count, we were a month coming from Percé to Quebec. That was because we were sailing against this same autumn wind which will be carrying *La Bonne Espérance* out to sea."

"But surely the aunts will have our letters by New Year's, and then they will know how glad I was of my béret and my jerseys, and how we can hardly wait to open the box up-

stairs. I can remember my Aunt Blanche a little, because she was young and pretty, and used to play with me. I suppose she is not young now, any more; it is eight years."

"Not young, exactly, but she will always have high spirits. And she is well married, and has three children who are a great joy to her."

"Three little cousins whom I have never seen, and one of them is named for me! Cécile, André, Rachel." She spoke their names softly. These little cousins were almost like playfellows. Their mother wrote such long letters about them that Cécile felt she knew them and all their ways, their individual faults and merits. Cousin Cécile was seven, very studious, *bien sérieuse*, already prepared for confirmation; but she would eat only sweets and highly spiced food. André was five, truthful and courageous, but he bit his nails. Rachel was a baby, in the midst of teething when they last heard of her.

Cécile would have preferred to live with Aunt Blanche and her children when she should go back to France; but by her mother's wish she was destined for Aunt Clothilde, who had long been a widow of handsome means and was much interested in the education of young girls. The face of this aunt Cécile could never remember, though she could see her figure clearly,—standing against the light, she always seemed to be, a massive woman, short and heavy though not exactly fat,—square, rather, like a great piece of oak furniture; always in black, widow's black that smelled of dye, with gold rings on her fingers and a very white handkerchief in her hand. Cécile could see her head, too, carried well back on a short neck, like a general or a statesman sitting for his portrait; but the face was a blank, just as if the aunt were standing in a doorway with blinding sunlight behind her. Cécile was once more trying to recall that face when her father interrupted her.

---

made the ménage   kept the household
tureen   big bowl
La Bonne Espérance   The Good Hope
tedious   dull
béret   a French cap

merit   strength, good point
bien sérieuse   very serious
confirmation   a ceremony to welcome young people formally into their religion

Think It Over

1. Why do you think Cécile and her father were so interested in the comings and goings of boats between France and Quebec?

2. Why do you suppose Cécile was planning to go back to France to go to school?

Literature
★ ★ ★ ★ ★ ★

CANADA

"Hatchet"

by Gary Paulsen

In the first summer after his parents' divorce, 13-year-old Brian flew in a tiny airplane to visit his father in Canada. As he and the pilot crossed over endless Canadian forests, the pilot suffered a heart attack and died. Brian had to land the plane on his own. He found himself near a lake deep in the forest. His only tool was a hatchet. Here, Brian struggles to make fire.

Brian found it was a long way from sparks to fire. Clearly there had to be something for the sparks to ignite, some kind of tinder or kindling—but what? He brought some dried grass in, tapped sparks into it and watched them die. He tried small twigs, breaking them into little pieces, but that was worse than the grass. Then he tried a combination of the two, grass and twigs.

Nothing. He had no trouble getting sparks, but the tiny bits of hot stone or metal—he couldn't tell which they were—just sputtered and died.

He settled back on his haunches in exasperation, looking at the pitiful clump of grass and twigs.

He needed something finer, something soft and fine and fluffy to catch the bits of fire.

Shredded paper would be nice, but he had no paper.

"So close," he said aloud, "so close . . ."

He put the hatchet back in his belt and went out of the shelter, limping on his sore leg. There had to be something, had to be. Man had made fire. There had been fire for thousands, millions of years. There had to be a way. He dug in his pockets and found the twenty-dollar bill in his wallet. Paper. Worthless paper out here. But if he could get a fire going . . .

He ripped the twenty into tiny pieces, made a pile of pieces, and hit sparks into them. Nothing happened. They just wouldn't take the sparks. But there had to be a way—some way to do it.

Not twenty feet to his right, leaning out over the water were birches and he stood looking at them for a full half-minute before they registered on his mind. They were a beautiful white with bark like clean, slightly speckled paper.

Paper.

He moved to the trees. Where the bark was peeling from the trunks it lifted in tiny tendrils, almost fluffs. Brian plucked some of them loose, rolled them in his fingers. They seemed flammable, dry and nearly powdery. He pulled and twisted bits off the trees, packing them in one hand while he picked them with the other, picking and gathering until he had a wad close to the size of a baseball.

Then he went back into the shelter and arranged the ball of birchbark peelings at the base of the black rock. As an afterthought he threw in the remains of the twenty-dollar bill. He struck and a stream of sparks fell into the bark and quickly died. But this time one spark fell on one small hair of dry bark—almost a thread of bark—and seemed to glow a bit brighter before it died.

The material had to be finer. There had to be a soft and incredibly fine nest for the sparks.

I must make a home for the sparks, he thought. A perfect home or they won't stay, they won't make fire.

He started ripping the bark, using his fingernails at first, and when that didn't work he used the sharp edge of the hatchet, cutting the bark in thin slivers, hairs so fine they were almost not there. It was painstaking work, slow work, and he stayed with it for over two hours. Twice he stopped for a handful of berries and once to go to the lake for a drink. Then back to work, the sun on

tinder   things that help a fire burn

flammable   able to burn

his back, until at last he had a ball of fluff as big as a grapefruit—dry birchbark fluff.

He positioned his spark nest—as he thought of it—at the base of the rock, used his thumb to make a small depression in the middle, and slammed the back of the hatchet down across the black rock. A cloud of sparks rained down, most of them missing the nest, but some, perhaps thirty or so, hit in the depression and of those six or seven found fuel and grew, smoldered and caused the bark to take on the red glow.

Then they went out.

Close—he was close. He repositioned the nest, made a new and smaller dent with his thumb, and struck again.

More sparks, a slight glow, then nothing.

It's me, he thought. I'm doing something wrong. I do not know this—a cave dweller would have had a fire by now, a Cro-Magnon man would have a fire by now—but I don't know this. I don't know how to make a fire.

Maybe not enough sparks. He settled the nest in place once more and hit the rock with a series of blows, as fast as he could. The sparks poured like a golden waterfall. At first they seemed to take, there were several, many sparks that found life and took briefly, but they all died.

Starved.

He leaned back. They are like me. They are starving. It wasn't quantity, there were plenty of sparks, but they needed more.

I would kill, he thought suddenly, for a book of matches. Just one book. Just one match. I would kill.

What makes fire? He thought back to school. To all those science classes. Had he ever learned what made a fire? Did a teacher ever stand up there and say, "This is what makes a fire . . ."

He shook his head, tried to focus his thoughts. What did it take? You have to have fuel, he thought—and he had that. The bark was fuel. Oxygen—there had to be air.

He needed to add air. He had to fan on it, blow on it.

He made the nest ready again, held the hatchet backward, tensed, and struck four quick blows. Sparks came down and he leaned forward as fast as he could and blew.

Too hard. There was a bright, almost intense glow, then it was gone. He had blown it out.

Another set of strikes, more sparks. He leaned and blew, but gently this time, holding back and aiming the stream of air from his mouth to hit the brightest spot. Five or six sparks had fallen in a tight mass of bark hair and Brian centered his efforts there.

The sparks grew with his gentle breath. The red glow moved from the sparks themselves into the bark, moved and grew and became worms, glowing red worms that crawled up the bark hairs and caught other threads of bark and grew until there was a pocket of red as big as a quarter, a glowing red coal of heat.

And when he ran out of breath and paused to inhale, the red ball suddenly burst into flame.

"Fire!" He yelled. "I've got fire! I've got it, I've got it, I've got it . . ."

But the flames were thick and oily and burning fast, consuming the ball of bark as fast as if it were gasoline. He had to feed the flames, keep them going. Working as fast as he could he carefully placed the dried grass and wood pieces he had tried at first on top of the bark and was gratified to see them take.

But they would go fast. He needed more, and more. He could not let the flames go out.

He ran from the shelter to the pines and started breaking off the low, dead small limbs. These he threw in the shelter, went back for more, threw those in, and squatted to break and feed the hungry flames. When the small wood was going well he went out and found larger wood and did not relax until that was going. Then he leaned back against the wood brace of his door opening and smiled.

I have a friend, he thought—I have a friend now. A hungry friend, but a good one. I have a friend named fire.

"Hello, fire . . ."

repositioned   put into position again

The curve of the rock back made an almost perfect drawing flue that carried the smoke up through the cracks of the roof but held the heat. If he kept the fire small it would be perfect and would keep anything like the porcupine from coming through the door again.

A friend and a guard, he thought.

So much from a little spark. A friend and a guard from a tiny spark.

He looked around and wished he had somebody to tell this thing, to show this thing he had done. But there was nobody.

Nothing but the trees and the sun and the breeze and the lake.

Nobody.

Think It Over

1. Why was it so important for Brian to create fire? What tasks and goals would fire help him do? How would fire make Brian's time in the wilderness different?

2. One feeling Brian had after he created the fire was pride. What else might he have felt?

BRITISH COLUMBIA, CANADA

from *A Child in Prison Camp*
by Shizuye Takashima

During World War II, when Canada was at war with Japan, Japanese Canadians were feared as possible enemies. The Canadian government sent them from their homes to camps where they stayed for several years. Here, Shizuye Takashima's journal describes the experiences of her family.

Japan is at war with the United States, Great Britain, and all the Allied Countries, including Canada, the country of my birth. My parents are Japanese, born in Japan, but they have been Canadian citizens for many, many years and have become part of this young country. Now, overnight, our rights as Canadians are taken away. Mass evacuation for the Japanese!

"All the Japanese," it is carefully explained to me, "whether we were born in Tokyo or in Vancouver are to be moved to distant places. Away from the west coast of British Columbia—for security reasons."

We must all leave—my sister Yuki, my older brother David, my parents, our relatives—all.

The older men are the first to go. The Government feels that my father, or his friends, might sabotage the police and their buildings. Imagine! I couldn't believe such stories, but there is my father packing just his clothes in a small suitcase.

Yuki says, "They are going to the foothills of the Rockies, to Tête Jaune. No one's there, and I guess they feel Father won't bomb the mountains."

The older people are very frightened. Mother is so upset; so are all her friends. I, being only eleven, seem to be on the outside.

One March day, we go to the station to see Father board the train. . . .

We have been waiting for months now. The Provincial Government keeps changing the dates of our evacuation, first from April, then from June, for different reasons: lack of trains, the camps are not ready. We are given another final notice. We dare not believe this is the one.

Mother is anxious. She has just received a letter from Father that he is leaving his camp with others; the families will be back together. I feel happy. He writes that he is located in one of the most beautiful spots in British Columbia. It's near a small village, 1800 feet above sea level. The Government wants the Japanese to build their own sanatorium for the T.B. patients. I hear there are many Japanese who have this disease, and the high altitude and dry air are supposed to be good for them. I feel secretly happy, for I love the mountains. I shall miss the roaring sea, but we are to be near a lake. Yuki says, "They decided all the male heads of families are to rejoin their wives, but the single men stay." So, of course, David will remain in his camp, far away.

We rise early, very early, the morning we are to leave. The city still sleeps. The fresh autumn air feels nice. We have orders to be at the Exhibition Grounds. The train will leave from there, not from the station where we said good-bye to Father and to David. We wait for the train in small groups scattered alongside the track. There is no platform. It is September 16. School has started. I think of my school friends and wonder if I shall ever see them again. The familiar mountains, all purple and splendid, watch us from afar. The yellowy-orangy sun slowly appears. We have been standing for over an hour. The sun's warm rays reach us, touch a child still

Allied Countries countries, including Canada and the United States, who fought against Germany, Japan, and Italy during World War II
evacuation being removed from one's home

sabotage lay a trap, damage
sanatorium health clinic
T.B. tuberculosis, a disease of the lungs

sleeping in its mother's arms, touch a tree, blades of grass. All seems magical. I study the thin, yellow rays of the sun. I imagine a handsome prince will come and carry us all away in a shining, gold carriage with white horses. I daydream and feel nice as long as I don't think about leaving this city where I was born.

The crisp air becomes warmer. I shift my feet, restless. Mother returns; she has been speaking to her friend. "Everyone says we will have to wait for hours." She bends, moves the bundles at our feet: food, clothes for the journey. I am excited. This is my first train ride! Yuki smiles. She, too, feels the excitement of our journey. Several children cry, weary of waiting. Their mothers' voices are heard, scolding.

Now the orange sun is far above our heads. I hear the twelve o'clock whistle blow from a nearby factory. Yuki asks me if I am tired. I nod. "I don't feel tired yet, but I'm getting hungry." We haven't eaten since six in the morning. Names are being called over the loudspeaker. One by one, families gather their belongings and move toward the train. Finally ours is called.

Yuki shouts, "That's us!"

granaries   buildings used in grain harvesting

I shout, "Hooray!" I take a small bag; Yuki and Mother, the larger ones and the suitcases. People stare as we walk toward the train. It is some distance away. I see the black, dull-colored train. It looks quite old. Somehow I had expected a shiny new one.

Yuki remarks, "I hope it moves. You never know with the Government."

Mother looks, smiles. "Never mind, as long as we get there. We aren't going on a vacation; we are being evacuated."

Bang . . . bang . . . psst . . . the old train gurgles, makes funny noises. I, seated by the window, feel the wheels move, stop, move, stop. Finally I hear them begin to move in an even rhythm slowly.

I look out the dusty window. A number of people still wait their turn. We wave. Children run after the train. Gradually it picks up speed. We pass the gray granaries, tall and thin against the blue Vancouver sky. The far mountains and tall pines follow us for a long time until finally they are gone.

Mother sits opposite; she has her eyes closed, her hands are on her lap. Yuki stares out the window. A woman across the aisle quietly dabs her tears with white cloth. No one speaks.

Think It Over

1. How did Shizuye feel about the evacuation? Why do you think she had so many different feelings?

2. In time of war, why might a government want to keep its coastline secure?

3. Was the internment of the Japanese Canadians fair? Was it necessary? Why do you think so?

Name _____   Date _____

ENGLAND
"A Women's Prison in London"
from *The Journal of Flora Tristan* translated by Jean Hawkes

Flora Tristan was the niece of Peru's president. Her father was an officer in the Peruvian Spanish army. But after her father's death, Flora lived in Europe with her mother. They were poor, and they struggled without the support of the wealthier Peruvian part of the family. Flora's early hardships helped her sympathize with the horrors facing women in London's Newgate prison, which she visited in 1841. She wrote this letter describing her visit.

I confess I felt very ill at ease in this lodge. There is no fresh air or daylight; the prisoner can still hear the noise of the street outside, and beneath the door he can still see the sunlight shining in the square. What a dreadful contrast, and how he regrets the loss of his liberty! But once past the lodge he hears nothing more; the atmosphere is as cold, damp and heavy as in a cellar; most of the passages are narrow, and so are the stairs leading to the upper wards.

First I was taken to see the women's wing. Over the past few years several changes have been made at Newgate and now it houses only prisoners awaiting trial, not convicted prisoners; in this respect it corresponds to the Conciergerie in Paris. It is here too that most executions take place.

The internal arrangement of the prison is not very satisfactory and there is not enough space for individual cells. In each ward the beds, wooden constructions six feet long and two feet wide, are arranged in two or three tiers like berths on board a ship. There is a large table in the middle with wooden benches all round it; this is where the prisoners eat, work, read and write. On close examination I found the wards very clean and well-kept, but as they are dark and poorly ventilated and the floors are very uneven, their general appearance is unpleasing.

Nearly all the women I saw there were of the lowest class. . . . Four were on charges carrying the death penalty for crimes classified as felonies under English law. Most of them seemed to be of low intelligence, but I noticed several whose tight thin lips, pointed nose, sharp chin, deep-set eyes and sly look I took as signs of exceptional depravity. I saw only one woman there who aroused my interest. She was confined with six others in a dark, damp low-ceilinged cell; when we entered they all rose and made us the customary servile curtsey which had embarrassed and irritated me from the moment I set foot in the prison. One alone refrained and it was this sign of independence which attracted my attention. Picture a young woman of twenty-four, small, well-made and tastefully dressed, standing with head held high to reveal a perfect profile, graceful neck. My eyes filled with tears and only the presence of the governor prevented me from going up to her and taking her hand so that she might understand my interest in her fate and so that my sympathy might calm for a few moments the sufferings of her heart.

Beauty can only be supreme when it reflects the noblest qualities of the soul. Without that inner radiance even the most beautiful woman in that sad place would have left me unmoved; but there was such dignity in this beauty which bore the depths of misfortune with pride and courage.

lodge   building at the gate
corresponds to   is the same as
internal arrangement   layout of the rooms, floor plan
ward   large room or group of rooms housing several people
tier   layer
berth   bed

ventilated   aired
felonies   serious crimes
depravity   bad character, lack of morals
servile curtsey   a bow of politeness, here performed with false courtesy
governor   head of the prison
bore   withstood

Think It Over

1. What is one reason Flora Tristan might have been sympathetic to the young woman prisoner? How might the prisoner's situation remind Flora of her own childhood sufferings?

2. Several South American countries won their independence from Spain during the early 1800's. Why might these events make liberty an especially important issue for Flora and others of her time?

Name _____ Date _____

GEOGRAPHY

ENGLAND

Captain Scott's Letter to the British Public
by Captain Robert Falcon Scott

Suppose you had worked for years to reach a certain goal. How might you feel if you knew your efforts would fail? In January of 1912, Captain Robert Scott of the British Navy and his group of explorers reached the South Pole. They expected to be the first to get there. After discovering that another group had been first to reach the historic spot, they started home in low spirits. The journey ended in tragedy. Food ran out, and it was very cold. Scott and his companions died on the Antarctic ice. Their bodies were not found for eight months. With Scott's body was his travel diary in which he had written this last letter to the people of his country.

The causes of the disaster are due not to faulty organisation, but to the misfortune in all risks which had to be undertaken.

1. The loss of pony transport in March 1911 obliged me to start later than I had intended, and obliged the limits of stuff transported to be narrowed.

2. The weather throughout the outward journey, and especially the long gale in 83° S., stopped us.

3. The soft snow in lower reaches of glacier again reduced pace.

We fought these untoward events with a will and conquered, but it cut into our provision reserve.

Every detail of our food supplies, clothing and depôts made on the interior ice-sheet and over that long stretch of 700 miles to the Pole and back, worked out to perfection. The advance party would have returned to the glacier in fine form and with surplus of food, but for the astonishing failure of the man whom we had least expected to fail. Edgar Evans was thought the strongest man of the party.

The Beardmore Glacier is not difficult in fine weather, but on our return we did not get a single completely fine day; this with a sick companion enormously increased our anxieties.

As I have said elsewhere we got into frightfully rough ice and Edgar Evans received a concussion of the brain—he died a natural death, but left us a shaken party with the season unduly advanced.

But all the facts above enumerated were as nothing to the surprise which awaited us on the Barrier. I maintain that our arrangements for returning were quite adequate, and that no one in the world would have expected the temperatures and surfaces which we encountered at this time of the year. On the summit in lat. 85° 86° we had –20°, –30°. On the Barrier in lat. 80°, 10,000 feet lower, we had –30° in the day, –47° at night pretty regularly, with continuous head wind during our day marches. It is clear that these circumstances come on very suddenly, and our wreck is certainly due to this sudden advent of severe weather, which does not seem to have any satisfactory cause. I do not think human beings ever came through such a month as we have come through, and we should have got through in spite of the weather but for the sickening of a second companion, Captain Oates, and a shortage of fuel in our depôts for which I cannot account, and finally, but for the storm which has fallen on us within 11

faulty   mistaken, flawed
obliged   required
gale   strong winds
glacier   permanent but slow-moving ice
untoward   unexpected and unwelcome
depôts   staging areas for storing food and supplies at points along the journey so as to avoid carrying too much

concussion   severe injury from a hard blow
unduly   unexpectedly
enumerated   listed one at a time
advent   arrival

miles of the depôt at which we hoped to secure our final supplies.

Surely misfortune could scarcely have exceeded this last blow. We arrived within 11 miles of our old One Ton Camp with fuel for one last meal and food for two days.

For four days we have been unable to leave the tent—the gale howling about us. We are weak, writing is difficult, but for my own sake I do not regret this journey, which has shown that Englishmen can endure hardships, help one another, and meet death with as great a fortitude as ever in the past. We took risks, we knew we took them; things have come out against us, and therefore we have no cause for complaint, but bow to the will of Providence, determined still to do our best to the last. But if we have been willing to give our lives to this enterprise, which is for the honour of our country, I appeal to our countrymen to see that those who depend upon us are properly cared for.

Had we lived, I should have had a tale to tell of the hardihood, endurance, and courage of my companions which would have stirred the heart of every Englishmen. These rough notes and our dead bodies must tell the tale, but surely, surely, a great rich country like ours will see that those who are dependent on us are properly provided for.

—*R. Scott*

fortitude bravery, strength

hardihood strength, endurance

Think It Over

1. Why didn't Captain Scott's preparations to protect himself and his party from the weather succeed?

2. What do you think Captain Scott was asking of the British people? How do you think they may have responded?

Name _____ Date _____

FRANCE

A Letter
by Blaise Pascal

About 150 years after Leonardo da Vinci's scientific experiments, Renaissance science was still moving forward.
Scientists had developed new ways to test their ideas. One
method was by repeated experiment. Here is a letter written by scientist and thinker Blaise Pascal, in which he
asked his brother-in-law to help him test the idea that air
has a different pressure as elevation increases.

November 15, 1647

I am taking the liberty of interrupting you in your daily professional labors, and of bothering you with questions of physics, because I know that they provide rest and recreation for your
moments of leisure. . . . The question concerns the well-known
experiment carried out with a tube containing mercury, first at
the foot and then at the top of a mountain, and repeated several
times on the same day, in order to ascertain whether the height of
the column of mercury is the same or differs in the two cases. . . .
For it is certain that at the foot of the mountain the air is much
heavier than at the top.

physics the study of energy and matter
tube . . . mercury mercury is a liquid metallic element that reacts to changes in
  temperature or air pressure
ascertain determine, figure out

Think It Over

1. What exactly was Pascal asking his brother-in-law to
   do? What can you conclude from this letter about the
   way science was conducted in the 1600's?

2. When reporting the successful proving of Pascal's theory, the brother-in-law later wrote that he was filled
   with "wonder and admiration." Why do you think he
   felt that way about Pascal's discovery?

FRANCE

A Letter
by Bishop Fulbert of Chartres

Which do you think is a harder job, worker or boss? Perhaps each has its challenges. During medieval times, the bosses were the lords and the workers were called vassals. The feudal system defined a contract between the lord and his vassals. Both sides of the contract had duties to the other. This letter was written in 1020. It describes some of those duties.

He who takes the oath of fealty to his lord ought always to keep in mind these six things: what is harmless, safe, honorable, useful, easy, and practicable. *Harmless*, which means that [the vassal] ought not to injure his lord in his body; *safe*, that [the vassal] should not injure [the lord] by betraying his confidence [trust] or the defenses upon which he depends for security; *honorable*, that [the vassal] should not injure [the lord] . . . in matters that relate to [the lord's] honor; *useful*, that [the vassal] should not injure [the lord's] . . . property; *easy*, that [the vassal] should not make difficult that which his lord can do easily; and *practicable*, that [the vassal] should not make impossible for the lord that which is possible.

However, while it is proper that the faithful vassal avoid these injuries, it is not for doing this alone that he deserves his holding; for it is not enough to refrain from wrongdoing, unless that which is good is done also. . . . Therefore, . . . in the same six things referred to above he should faithfully advise and aid his lord, if he wishes to . . . be safe concerning his fealty which he has sworn.

The lord also ought to act toward his faithful vassal in the same manner in all these things. And if he fails to do this, he will be rightfully regarded as guilty of bad faith, just as the former [would be], if he should be found shirking . . . his obligations."

oath of fealty   promise of loyalty
betraying his confidence   breaking his trust
shirking   avoiding, failing to fill

Think It Over

1. What characteristic in people do you think the feudal system valued most? Why was this so important to that society?

2. How are the duties of lords and vassals to each other similar? How are they different?

ITALY

A Letter
by Leonardo da Vinci

Do you know what you do best? If you were listing the abilities later generations would remember you had, what would be first and last on the list? Leonardo da Vinci was an extraordinary man of many talents, but it is surprising to see which ones he thought were most important. Leonardo is one of the best known figures from the Renaissance. During that time in Europe, many changes took place in thinking, art, and science. In this letter, Leonardo is applying to the Duke of Milan for a job. Notice that he lists his painting and sculpture abilities, which we now remember him so well for, at the bottom of the list.

Having, most illustrious lord, seen and considered the experiments of all those who pose as masters in the art of inventing instruments of war, and finding that their inventions differ in no way from those in common use, I am emboldened, without prejudice to anyone, to solicit an appointment of acquainting your Excellency with certain of my secrets.

1. I can construct bridges which are very light and strong and very portable, with which to pursue and defeat the enemy; and others more solid, which resist fire or assault, yet are easily removed and placed in position; and I can also burn and destroy those of the enemy.

2. In case of a siege I can cut off water from the trenches and make pontoons and scaling ladders and other similar contrivances.

3. If by reason of the elevation or the strength of its position a place cannot be bombarded, I can demolish every fortress if its foundations have not been set on stone.

4. I can also make a kind of cannon which is light and easy of transport, with which to hurl small stones like hail, and of which the smoke causes great terror to the enemy, so that they suffer heavy loss and confusion.

5. I can noiselessly construct to any prescribed point subterranean passages either straight or winding, passing if necessary underneath trenches or a river.

6. I can make armoured wagons carrying artillery, which shall break through the most serried ranks of the enemy, and so open a safe passage for his infantry.

7. If occasion should arise, I can construct cannon and mortars and light ordnance in shape both ornamental and useful and different from those in common use.

8. When it is impossible to use cannon I can supply in their stead catapults, mangonels, trabocchi, and other instruments of admirable efficiency not in general use—In short, as the occasion requires I can supply infinite means of attack and defense.

9. And if the fight should take place upon the sea I can construct many engines most suitable either for attack or defense and ships which can resist the fire of the heaviest cannon, and powders or weapons.

10. In time of peace, I believe that I can give you as complete satisfaction as anyone

illustrious   well-known
pose   pretend to be
emboldened   made brave
prejudice   promise or restriction
solicit   ask for
siege   attack
pontoon   float used to hold up a floating bridge
scaling ladder   ladder for climbing walls or cliffs
contrivances   tools, machines, pieces of equipment
bombarded   reached with weapons
demolish   destroy

subterranean   underground
artillery   weapons for shooting flying objects, for example, a cannon
serried   crowded
infantry   foot soldiers
ordnance   various supplies for soldiers, including bullets
catapults, mangonels, trabocchi   large weapons often used to shoot missile-like objects at the enemy from a great distance

else in the construction of buildings both public and private, and in conducting water from one place to another.

I can further execute sculpture in marble, bronze or clay, also in painting I can do as much as anyone else, whoever he may be.

Moreover, I would undertake the commission of the bronze horse, which shall endue with immortal glory and eternal hon-our the auspicious memory of your father and of the illustrious house of Sforza.———

And if any of the aforesaid things should seem to anyone impossible or impracticable, I offer myself as ready to make trial of them in your park or in whatever place shall please your Excellency, to whom I commend myself with all possible humility.

endue with give to
auspicious having good fortune

aforesaid said before
impracticable not realistic to do

Think It Over

1. How do you think Leonardo viewed himself? Do you think he was proud of his abilities? Why or why not?

2. Why do you think Leonardo listed his military inventions first?

Literature
★ ★ ★ ★ ★

DENMARK

"The Boy"

from *The Untold Tale* by Erik Christian Haugaard

It was the mid-1600's. Denmark was at war with Sweden, and life in the countryside was harsh. In this story, the long northern winter had come, and Dag's family was starving. His father had gone in search of charity to save the family. Dag remained behind with his sick mother and a shrinking group of animals. Faced with great responsibilities, Dag must act grown up or surely die.

The boy knelt on the bench trying to look through the little window into the yard of the farm; but the glass was so poor that he could hardly see through it, and it acted as a mirror. The boy moved his face just slightly and now his reflection had four eyes. He smiled and cocked his head and he had two noses like a witch.

It was an old game and he soon grew tired of it. He climbed down from the bench. In a corner of the room, near the open fireplace, was a tiny shelf where his playthings were kept. He took down one of the flint stones that he had found the summer before, when he had gone with his father to gather seaweed at a beach. The sea had worn a hole through the stone. The boy stuck his little finger through the hole. He had eight such stones. They were different sizes, and each represented an animal. The two larger ones were a team of horses; the others were cows and sheep. When he played out of doors, he tied a string through the holes and tethered his animals in the field. Each of his stone animals had a name and he knew its particular nature. The largest stone was a stallion; it was willful, liable to break its tether and run away.

He heard the barn door bang; it must have blown open. He knew that he ought to go out and shut it. He put his stones away but he remained in the room. He was afraid to go out to the stable, for he had been there in the morning and found the gelding dead. Its eyes had been all white.

He walked back to the table and sat down on the bench. He looked at his hands and carefully counted his fingers, as if he expected to have lost one. He broke the silence of the room by whispering, "Mother . . ." But the dying woman in the bed alcove did not hear him. He said the word again, a little louder; then he rose and tiptoed to the bed.

He stood still gazing at his mother; she appeared so small, as if she were a child now, too. He touched her cheek gently. She seemed cold to his touch, and yet her forehead was bathed in sweat. Slowly his mother opened her eyes and whispered his name. He shouted: "Mother!" But she turned her head towards the wall.

Again he heard the banging of the door and this time he went out to close it.

He need not have looked inside. He could just have closed the door and let the wooden latch fall into place. But once he had looked, he had had to enter. The young horse was still lying where it had fallen, its neck outstretched; all the bones of its body were visible through its skin. He could hear the breathing of the two cows who were still alive, but he did not dare approach them. He looked about for something to feed them. There was nothing, not even a handful of chaff. He noticed the straw roof, and the idea occurred to him of tearing out some straw and giving it to the cows.

He climbed the ladder to the loft; it was empty, swept clean even of dust. With his hands, he tore at the roof. It was old and the straw crumbled into ragged bits. Carefully, he collected an armful, taking small amounts from several different places, in order not to destroy the roof.

chaff   outer skin of grain such as wheat, left over after the seed has been removed by threshing

He climbed down into the stable. Both the cows were lying down. The boy divided the straw and put a bundle next to each cow's head. Neither of them made any attempt to rise; they were too weak to take any interest in dry dust.

When he came outside, the boy looked up at the blue sky; spring really was on its way. The icicles still hung from the eaves; but the sun had gained strength enough to make its warmth felt. The boy broke off a long, pointed icicle and sucked on it. He had not eaten since the day before; his father had made a gruel of barley before he had left for Elsinore. Dag wondered whether there might be something left in the pot; and even though he knew there wasn't, he returned to the house to look.

The pot was empty; he had scraped it himself that morning. He put a few sticks on top of the ashes that hid the embers and blew until they caught fire. He emptied water from the earthen pitcher into the iron pot, and hung the pot on the hook above the fire; though there was no reason to boil water, for he had nothing with which to make either soup or gruel.

Thinking that his mother might want something to drink, he filled his father's tin cup with water. Her face was still turned towards the wall. He called to her and when she did not answer, he bent forward and touched her.

Her eyes told him that she was dead; they were like the cow's had been when she died: empty. He tried to put the cup down on the table carefully, but even though it was not filled to the brim, he spilled a little of the water. He dried it up with his sleeve. Tears ran from his eyes, but he cried soundlessly. Twice he called out: "Mother . . . Mother . . ." But in the tone of his voice there was neither expectancy nor hope. Then he screamed: "Father!" and ran out of the house pursued by his own fear.

He ran as quickly as he could past the two neighboring farms, that had been abandoned not long after New Year. When he reached the great forest, the sun was low on the horizon and the darkness of the woods frightened him. Reluctantly, he started back to the farm; but then he thought that he might have been wrong: that his mother might not be dead, and he started to run.

He entered the house out of breath. In the silence of the room, he could hear his own heart beating and he knew that he had not been mistaken. He did not walk to the alcove but to the fireplace. He looked into the iron pot; and since the water had boiled away, he filled it. With great care he rebuilt the fire. He did everything slowly, wanting it to take time.

He sat by the fire all night, waiting and listening for his father's footsteps. Once he heard an owl hooting. The sound came down through the chimney into the room; he closed his eyes and shuddered, although his father had told him that it was not true that owls were the souls of dead people.

When the first grey light of morning came, he fell asleep on his little stool, his head resting in his hands. He slept until the middle of the morning when melting snow, falling from the roof into the yard, awakened him.

Without looking around the room, he hurried outside. The sun was so bright that it almost blinded him, and the sky was clear. There were hardly any icicles hanging from the eaves; the smashed bits of once foot-long cones lay glistening on the ground. The boy ran down to the pond; the ice was so soft that he was able to make marks in it with a stick.

Suddenly, as he stared at the lines he had been drawing in the ice, he felt certain that his father would not come back. He started to cry. Where was he to go? Who would help him? He looked over his shoulder towards the house; a little smoke was coming from the chimney. He had tried to pray during the night; but he knew only two prayers: the one you said before going to bed and the one of thanks recited before meals.

High above in the sky a lone swan was flying; Dag heard the beat of the wings. He dried his eyes and raised his head to look at it. "My father is dead," he said aloud. Then it was that it occurred to him to go and tell the King what had happened. His father had rented his land from the Crown, but the King was far away. "He doesn't know that we're starving!" the boy almost shouted. He—Dag—would tell King Christian of their misery and the King would help him. By some kind of miracle, the King would set all things right again; his mother and father would be alive and the mare and the gelding and the cows would be well. Everything would be as it had been last summer—no! as it had been last spring, before the drought.

He ran back to the house to make himself ready for his journey. His first thought was to find something in which to carry his stones; then he decided to take only the best one, the stallion. A moment later he told himself that he was foolish, and he was so ashamed that he took all the stones and dumped them into the well.

He was wearing his warmest clothes and his boots. After finding his knitted cap, he looked around the room, though his glance carefully avoided the alcove bed. He wanted to take the large knife, but it had no sheath and he wondered how he could carry it. What he needed was a piece of rope, and when he found one, he tied it around his tunic and stuck the knife into it. His father's tin spoon fitted nicely beside the knife. He

tunic   a very long shirt, which may be belted at the waist and worn over other clothes

was determined to take the tin cup as well, but he did not want to carry it in his hand; finally, he shoved the cup inside his tunic. His father's staff—the one he used to drive the animals—stood by the door; the boy grabbed it and found that he was ready. He opened the door and hesitated; but finally, he lifted his head and forced himself to glance at the alcove bed.

"I will come back, Mother," he called aloud. Then he walked out into the sunlight and closed the door behind him.

The boy stood in the middle of the farmyard holding the staff, which was twice his height, in his hand. He nodded to the house and to the barn, to say goodbye to them. Feeling that the moment was solemn, he dropped down on his knees in the wet snow and recited the prayer that he usually said before he got into bed. When he was almost finished, he remembered that he was wearing his cap, and he took it off. He was seven years old, Dag of King's Acre; and he was all alone.

A month later, the land was rented out again. A new farmer arrived with horses and cows. The body of Dag's mother was carried to the church at Gurre; and she was buried in the eastern part of the churchyard near the fence, farthest away from the church.

Think It Over

1. How did Dag feel after his mother's death?

2. In what ways did Dag's experiences change him? How did he grow up?

NORTHERN EUROPE
from *Maroo of the Winter Caves*
by Ann Turnbull

Ann Turnbull did a great deal of research to write a novel about people living at the end of the last Ice Age in Europe. In this excerpt, Maroo's father has been killed. She must help her family get to the winter camp where they will be safe from blizzards. Maroo's young brother Otak must save her when she is caught in an avalanche.

The glacier looked a smooth slate-blue in the dawn light. Maroo led the way, using her staff to prod the snow ahead of her before she set foot on it. She knew how unstable the glacier was; there could be vast crevasses under the firm-seeming snow.

"You must hold on to Rivo, and follow exactly in my footsteps," she told Otak.

The snow at the edge of the glacier was not so smooth as it looked; it was soft and powdery, dissolving under their feet to join the streams running down the mountain. As they moved on, it became firmer, but when Maroo looked back she saw their footprints like a row of small wells that would soon freeze over.

They went on, Maroo still moving ahead with her staff, prodding the snow to make sure it was firm. The snow was no longer soft and wet; it had hardened to a solid crust, or so it seemed, but they knew that the ice that looked so firm was slowly moving.

As they trekked in a long diagonal across the face of the glacier, Otak and Rivo followed obediently in Maroo's footsteps. Rivo sniffed and whined at the tracks of a hare, and Otak wanted to follow them, but Maroo said no, there could be no hunting until they were on firmer ground. To her relief, Otak obeyed after a moment's hesitation, pulling the dog's lead tight and plodding reluctantly along behind Maroo.

By midday they were more than halfway to the pass between the two peaks that Maroo had seen from far below. She began to feel confident that they would soon be safe. Both she and Otak were hungry, but they would not stop to eat until they were across the glacier.

Maroo looked up and saw the pass easily within reach, though the way up was steeper. She stepped forward, with the staff in her right hand. The snow crumbled a little under her left foot, and she felt a jolting movement. Before she could leap away, she was thrown violently sideways, there was a roar of cracking ice, and she felt herself falling. She screamed, clawing at the crumbling snow as she plunged down into a crevasse, an avalanche of snow and ice falling in on top of her.

At last it stopped. She lay still, too bruised and exhausted even to open her eyes. A great weight seemed to be pressing her down, urging her to sleep. When she did at last force herself to open her eyes, she moved in sudden panic, realizing that she was buried under the snow and would soon suffocate.

She tried to stand up, but the lower half of her body was trapped. She was not even sure which way was up—perhaps she was standing. Her arms and hands had some movement in them. She began to push up frantically at the snow, which was fast hardening over her. She seemed to be buried up to her neck, and it took all her strength to free the upper half of her body.

As she worked, a faint sound came to her from above. At first she did not react to

glacier   slow moving, permanent ice sheet
staff   long, strong stick

crevasses   deep cracks
trekked   hiked

it, absorbed as she was in her fight for life; then the sound penetrated, and she realized it was a voice: her brother's voice, calling her name. Tilting her head back as far as it would go, she squinted up at a patch of bright sky with a silhouette of a head in it.

"Otak!" she tried to call, but only a hoarse croak came out.

Something else appeared in the patch of blinding sky: something dark hurtling down. Instinctively she cringed, but it was not falling snow, it was a rope of plaited hide. Maroo heaved desperately with her legs, but they would not move. She began to dig with her hands, faster and faster, knowing that soon she would freeze and it would be too late. At last she was able to move part of her legs; then she felt life in one foot. She threw herself sideways and rolled over, freeing one leg and then the other, and ending up kneeling on all fours beside the rope. She crouched there, panting.

Her brother was shouting at her from the sky above, but the shouting did not seem real; it seemed to come from another world. "The rope!" Otak shouted. "Tie the rope!"

With a great effort Maroo shook off her exhaustion. She took hold of the rope and knotted it firmly around her waist. She felt a faint tug from above; was she ready? She doubted if she would have the strength to climb out, but she gave an answering tug on the rope, stood up, and braced herself against the side of the crevasse.

The rope went taut. Maroo began to claw her way up the wall of the crevasse, grunting with exertion. Several times the rope slackened, and she heard a cry of alarm from Otak. Otak was so much smaller and lighter than she was—how could he hold her? Her foot slipped, she jerked downward with a gasp of fear, Otak yelled, and she saw him clinging to the edge of the

crevasse and heard Rivo barking. In desperation she dug toeholds in the hard snow with her boots and clambered up, releasing the strain on Otak.

She looked up and saw the sky growing larger. Otak was there, his face hanging like a moon in the patch of blue. He shouted encouragement, but he looked frightened. Only a little farther now. With what felt like the last of her strength, Maroo dragged herself up until her hands touched his. He seized her wrists. She hauled herself up and out, and lay shaking on the ice. Rivo's wet tongue caressed her face.

When she had recovered enough to raise her head, she saw that Otak had driven his staff deep into the snow and wound the rope round it as well as around his own body to help take the strain. He untied the rope, coiled it neatly, and replaced it in his pack. Then he dropped down beside her, and she realized that they were both overcome with shock.

They crouched there, trembling, for some time, too tired to move, till Maroo said shakily, "We must go on—we dare not be trapped here at night."

She found her staff lying at the edge of the crevasse and picked it up. They both lifted their packs. Suddenly Otak touched Maroo's arm and pointed upward. There, on the pass between the two peaks, a big buck ibex was standing, quite unafraid, watching them. As they looked up, it turned and vanished over the brow of the hill.

Otak fixed wide, frightened eyes on his sister. Maroo felt her heart fluttering.

"Was it a spirit?" Otak asked.

"Maybe."

"Father's spirit?"

Maroo's heart beat faster. A vision came into her mind of Areg dead with the heavy stones laid on him to keep his spirit from walking.

silhouette outline
plaited braided
slackened loosened

caressed stroked, soothed
ibex animal similar to a deer or moose

"No," she said hastily. "Why should his spirit come so far?"

"To be with us?"

"No," Maroo insisted. But Old Mother had said that the mountain was guarded by spir-its, and Areg had been killed hunting an ibex. Firmly she put these thoughts out of her mind.

"We must go on," she repeated. "Whatever is up there, we must go on now."

Think It Over

1. Why was Maroo confused about which way to dig?

2. What do you think gave Maroo the strength to climb out of the crevasse?

Eyewitness Account ★★★★★★

GEOGRAPHY

FRANCE/RUSSIA

A Letter From Napoleon's Army
by Count Philippe-Paul de Ségur

In the early 1800's, Napoleon Bonaparte was the emperor of France. When he tried to invade Russia's city of Moscow, its residents burned the city and fled. Napoleon's army could get no supplies and had to retreat. They were caught in the bitter Russian winter, and many died of cold or starvation. This letter was written from the battlefield.

The Eighth of September

Napoleon rode over the battlefield; there was never such a ghastly sight. Everything contributed to the horror of it: the gloomy sky, the cold rain, the violent gale, the houses in ashes, the plain torn up, littered with ruins and debris. On the horizon the melancholy foliage of the northern trees; soldiers wandering among the corpses, looking for food in the very knapsacks of their fallen comrades; dreadful wounds (Russian bullets were larger than ours); cold campfires without song or tale; a tragic silence!

Clustered round the standards were the few remaining officers, noncommissioned officers, and soldiers—barely enough to guard the eagle. Their clothing was torn by the violence of the struggle, black with powder, stained with blood. Yet, despite the rags, the misery and disaster, they still looked proud and let out shouts of triumph at the sight of the Emperor. The shouts, though, were rare and excited; for in this army, capable of self-analysis as well as enthusiasm, each individual was aware of the total situation. French soldiers are not easily deceived; and these wondered why, with so many Russians killed and wounded, there should be only eight hundred prisoners. It was by the number of prisoners that they judged success, since the dead attested to the courage of the defeated, rather than to a victory. If the survivors were able to retreat in such good order, proud and undaunted, what did the winning of one field matter? In this vast country, would the Russians ever lack for space on which to fight?

The First Snowstorm

On the sixth of November the sky became terrible; its blue disappeared. The army marched along wrapped in a cold mist. Then the mist thickened, and presently from this immense cloud great snowflakes began to sift down on us. It seemed as if the sky had come down and joined with the earth and our enemies to complete our ruin. Everything in sight became vague, unrecognizable. Objects changed their shape; we walked without knowing where we were or what lay ahead, and anything became an obstacle. While the men were struggling to make headway against the icy, cutting blast, the snow driven by the wind was piling up and filling the hollows along the way. Their smooth surfaces hid unsuspected depths which opened up treacherously under our feet. The men were swallowed up, and the weak, unable to struggle out, were buried forever.

The soldiers following them turned around, but the tempest whipped their faces with the snow falling from above or swept up from the earth, and seemed fiercely determined to oppose their progress. Russian winter in this new guise attacked them on all sides; it cut through their thin uniforms and worn shoes, their wet clothing froze on them, and this icy shroud molded their bodies and

melancholy foliage   the trees of the far north are mostly evergreens with needles instead of leaves
standards   flags
noncommissioned officers   officers with less authority
self-analysis   thinking about the situation one is in

attested to   was proof of
undaunted   unbeaten, unafraid
tempest   storm
guise   form
shroud   a cloth used to cover a corpse before burial

Readings From Social Studies   **117**

stiffened their limbs. The sharp wind made them gasp for breath, and froze the moisture from their mouths and nostrils into icicles on their beards. . . .

But in front of them, all around them, everything was snow. The eyes of the men were lost in the immense, dreary uniformity. To their stricken imagination it was like a

great white shroud that Nature was winding about the army. The only objects that stood out were the tall somber firs, graveyard trees, as we called them, with the funereal verdure, and the gigantic immobility of their black trunks, which completed a picture of universal mourning, a dying army in the midst of a dead nature.

uniformity   sameness
stricken   weakened
funereal verdure   the bushes and trees seem very
  serious, like the mood at a funeral

immobility   inability to move

Think It Over

1. Why were the French soldiers surprised that there were only 800 Russian prisoners? What does this suggest about the outcome of the battle?

2. How did the geography of Russia help its soldiers? How did it hurt the French soldiers?

Name _____ Date _____

Lenin's Deathbed Words
by Vladimir Lenin

An important leader of the Bolshevik movement, Vladimir Lenin helped found the Soviet Union. There was a lot of fighting among different groups within the country as to how the new government should be run. As Lenin lay dying in the early 1920's, many people wanted to take over the power he would leave behind. In this postscript to a letter he wrote in January of 1925, Lenin warned the Soviet people about the danger he saw coming from one of those people, Joseph Stalin.

Postscript: Stalin is too rude, and this fault, entirely supportable in relations among us Communists, becomes insupportable in the office of General Secretary. Therefore, I propose to the comrades to find a way to remove Stalin from that position and appoint to it another man who in all respects differs from Stalin only in superiority—namely, more patient, more loyal, more polite and more attentive to comrades, less capricious, etc. This circumstance may seem an insignificant trifle, but I think that from the point of view of preventing a split and from the point of view of the relation between Stalin and Trotsky which I discussed above, it is not a trifle, or it is such a trifle as may acquire a decisive significance.

—*Lenin*

postscript new text added on to the end of a letter, containing an idea thought of at the last moment
supportable acceptable, supported by reason
comrades members of the Communist party
capricious likely to change his mind without warning or cause
trifle a little and unimportant thing
Trotsky another revolutionary, with whom Stalin was struggling for power
decisive important in deciding

RUSSIA

Kampf

by Joseph Stalin

Lenin turned out to be right about Joseph Stalin. He
was a brutal dictator who killed and jailed many Soviets.
The statement below suggests a little of his personality.

To choose one's victim, to prepare one's plans minutely, to
stake an implacable vengeance, and then to go to bed . . . there is
nothing sweeter in the world."

minutely   considering even the tiniest detail
implacable   horrible, without any possible relief
vengeance   revenge

RUSSIA

Housekeeping in Russia
Soon After the Revolution

by Marina Tsvetayeva

Revolution is never easy, especially for families. At first
poet Marina Tsvetayeva supported the Russian revolution.
But in 1919 she wrote to her sister and described the hardships she and her young children were suffering. Her husband, Seryozha, was missing and may have been jailed or
killed in the revolution.

I live with Alya and Irina (Alya is six, Irina two) in our same flat
opposite two trees in the attic room which used to be Seryozha's.
We have no flour and no bread. Under my writing desk there are
about twelve pounds of potatoes which is all that is left from the
food 'lent' by my neighbours. These are the only provisions we
have. I walk all over Moscow looking for bread. If Alya comes with
me, I have to tie Irina to a chair, for safety. I feed Irina, then put
her to bed. She sleeps in the blue armchair. There is a bed but it
won't go through the door. I boil up some old coffee, and drink it,
and have a smoke. I write. Alya writes or reads. There is silence
for two hours; then Irina wakes up. We heat up what remains of
the mashed goo. With Alya's help, I fish out the potatoes which
remain, or rather have become clogged in the bottom of the
samovar. Either Alya or myself puts Irina back to bed. Then Alya
goes to bed. At 10 pm the day is over.

flat   apartment
provisions   supplies
samovar   a closed pitcher used in Russia to heat up foods and drinks

CZECH REPUBLIC

A Speech

by Václav Havel

Communism didn't last very long as a way of government. By the late 1980's, the Soviet Union and its communist government were weakening. In 1990, the country of Czechoslovakia broke free of that influence. Writer Václav Havel was chosen to lead the new democratic government. He had been jailed three times for protesting the old government. Here is part of the speech he made as he took office.

My dear fellow citizens, for forty years on this day you heard from my predecessors the same thing in a number of variations: how our country is flourishing, how many millions of tons of steel we produce, how happy we all are, how we trust our government, and what bright prospects lie ahead of us.

I assume you did not propose me for this office so that I, too, should lie to you.

Our country is not flourishing. The enormous creative and spiritual potential of our nation is being wasted. Entire branches of industry produce goods that are of no interest to anyone, while we lack the things we need. The state, which calls itself a workers' state, humiliates and exploits workers. Our outmoded economy wastes what little energy we have. A country that once could be proud of the educational level of its citizens now spends so little on education that it ranks seventy-second in the world. We have polluted our land, rivers, and forests, bequeathed to us by our ancestors; we now have the most contaminated environment in all of Europe. People in our country die sooner than in the majority of European countries. . . .

You may ask what kind of republic I dream of. Let me reply: I dream of a republic that is independent, free, and democratic; a republic with economic prosperity yet social justice; a humane republic that serves the individual and therefore hopes that the individual will serve it in turn; a republic of well-rounded people, because without such people, it is impossible to solve any of our problems, whether they be human, economic, ecological, social, or political.

The most distinguished of my predecessors opened his first speech with a quote from Comenius [the great Czech educator of the seventeenth century]. Allow me to end my first speech with my own paraphrase of the same statement: My people, your government has returned to you!

predecessors   those who came before me
flourishing   thriving, succeeding
exploit   take advantage of, use without fair payment
outmoded   old fashioned
bequeathed   left to us

prosperity   success
humane   fair and kind to all people
paraphrase   saying someone else's idea or words in your own words

Think It Over

1. Lenin gives many reasons for disliking Stalin. What might be another reason for his attitude?

2. What qualities do you think are useful to people and their leaders during a revolution?

3. What do Václav Havel's comments suggest about the success of the communist revolution?

RUSSIA

from *The Endless Steppe*
by Esther Hautzig

Esther Hautzig was born and spent her early years in Vilna, Poland. In 1940, the Soviet army, which was then fighting in World War II alongside the Germans, invaded Vilna. Esther and her family were exiled to Siberia, along with many others. Here, Esther describes the harsh lands to which they were sent.

My first glimpse of Rubtsovsk was of a frontier village built around a large open square in straight lines, as if the muddy paths were laid out for ticktacktoe. Immediately surrounding the square were the market stalls, open wooden sheds. These were empty that day. Once again the loud-speaker crackled with authority; this time we were ordered to arrange ourselves in family groups in the square and await further instructions. Since families had clung to each other, this was done with dispatch.

The square was even hotter than the road, the sun being reflected from its cobblestones of all sizes and shapes. I stepped closer to my mother.

The flatness of this land was awesome. There wasn't a hill in sight; it was an enormous, unrippled sea of parched and lifeless grass.

"Tata, why is the earth so flat here?"

"These must be steppes, Esther."

"Steppes? But steppes are in Siberia."

"This is Siberia," he said quietly.

If I had been told that I had been transported to the moon, I could not have been more stunned.

"Siberia?" My voice trembled. "But Siberia is full of snow."

"It will be," my father said.

Siberia! Siberia was the end of the world, a point of no return. Siberia was for criminals and political enemies, where the punishment was unbelievably cruel, and where people died like flies. Summer or no summer—and who had ever talked about hot Siberia?—Siberia was the tundra and mountainous drifts of snow. Siberia was *wolves*.

I had been careless. I had neglected to pray to God to save us from a gypsum mine in Siberia.

Tata   Papa or Father
steppes   flat, treeless plains
tundra   far northern lands, treeless and with permanently frozen subsoil

gypsum   a mineral used in making plaster

Think It Over

1. What might it feel like to live in a place with no trees or hills?

2. Why was Esther so surprised to find it was hot in Siberia?

MOROCCO

from *Mokhtar of the Atlas Mountains*
by Elisabeth Thiebaut

The High Atlas Mountains of Morocco are home to the Ayt-Umdis, one group among the many Muslim Berber groups who live in Africa's far northwest. In the Ayt-Umdis village of Tawenzerft lives a boy named Mokhtar with his family. The villagers' main crop is walnuts. The money earned from selling these nuts is terribly important to the village. In this true story from Mokhtar's life, he has a dream warning of danger to the precious walnut crop.

Lulled by the singing of the birds, Mokhtar drifted off into a deep sleep. He had a dream. Flames were dancing around him and devouring the corn. It was hot and he was shouting in front of his burning home. At that moment a dead leaf fluttered down onto his eyelids and Mokhtar woke with a start. The nut tree started to shake. A flock of birds, twittering with fright, took to the air and a dark cloud passed over the old tree.

"The nut tree is warning me!" thought Mokhtar.

He leaped up and ran off as fast as his legs could carry him.

He crossed the fields, bounded over the ditch, climbed the path from the mosque and arrived at the house. A cloud of smoke was pouring out of the storeroom. Mokhtar forced the old wooden lock and pushed open the door. Already the fire was licking at the beams and threatening to attack the winter stores. Mokhtar climbed onto the flat roof and yelled at the top of his voice: "Fire! Fire!"

At once all the men, women and children working in the fields came running to help. Mokhtar ran into the main room and took the big jug of water. He went down to the storeroom and threw the water over the flames. Tudda arrived first and collected together all the jugs and pots in the house. The women rushed to the spring to fill them. They handed them to the men who threw the water onto the fire. Then the women filled the empty pots again.

At last the fire was under control. But the beams had been almost destroyed by the fire and looked as though they might give way. The winter stores, piled up in a corner, were almost untouched. Everyone looked at the damage in silence. Tudda and Zara were trying not to cry. Hasan drew the family together and said, "Bad luck has come upon our house, but don't cry. Tears won't rebuild houses. We must go to Ayt-Tamllil to tell the Ancient One and to ask the carpenter to come and repair the roof. Winter is coming and the provisions must be kept under cover."

Mokhtar looked up at his uncle, his eyes full of hope. Hasan hesitated for a moment then went on. "Mokhtar you're lucky. If you hadn't shouted, the house would have burned down. You can go to fetch them back."

Mokhtar went to find a mule. Tudda gave him her woolen cloak and two bread rolls and Brahim brought him some hay for the mule. Then he went up to his cousin. "Look," he said, "take my flashlight, it might be useful." Mokhtar took the flashlight gratefully, and put it in his leather bag. He had been to Ayt-Tamllil once with his father, but just to be sure Hasan went over the route in detail. Then he slapped the mule's neck and said, "Go! And may God go with you!"

devouring   destroying, eating up
mosque   Muslim house of worship

the Ancient One   Mokhtar's grandfather
provisions   foods and supplies stored for later use

Think It Over

1. Why do you think Mokhtar believed his dream was a warning? What does this suggest about his beliefs about dreams?

2. What do you think it would be like to wake up from a dream to find that events from the real world had appeared in your dream?

EGYPT

A Speech for Peace
by President Anwar el-Sadat

Since its founding after World War II, the Jewish state of Israel and its Arab neighbors had been enemies. Finally, during the 1970's, Egyptian President Anwar el-Sadat took a gigantic step for peace by traveling to Israel and speaking to the Knesset, the Israeli Parliament. Though he knew going to Israel was very dangerous for him, President el-Sadat also believed taking this risk would show the strength of his desire for peace. He was right. Important peace agreements were reached between the two nations in the 1970's. Anwar el-Sadat was assassinated in 1981.

I come to you today on solid ground to shape a new life and to establish peace. We all love this land, the land of God; we all, Moslems, Christians, and Jews, all worship God.

Under God, God's teachings and commandments are love, sincerity, security, and peace.

I do not blame all those who received my decision when I announced it to the entire world before the Egyptian People's Assembly. I do not blame all those who received my decision with surprise and even with amazement—some gripped even by violent surprise. Still others interpreted it as political, to camouflage my intentions of launching a new war.

I would go so far as to tell you that one of my aides at the presidential office contacted me at a late hour following my return home from the People's Assembly and sounded worried as he asked me, "Mr. President, what would be our reaction if Israel actually extended an invitation to you?"

I replied calmly, "I would accept it immediately. I have declared that I would go to the ends of the earth. I would go to Israel, for I want to put before the people of Israel all the facts."

I can see the faces of all those who were astounded by my decision and had doubts as to the sincerity of the intentions behind the declaration of my decision. No one could ever conceive that the president of the biggest Arab state, which bears the heaviest burden and the main responsibility pertaining to the cause of war and peace in the Middle East, should declare his readiness to go to the land of the adversary while we were still in a state of war. . . .

Here I would go back to the big question: How can we achieve a durable peace based on justice? In my opinion, and I declare it to the whole world, from this forum, the answer is neither difficult nor is it impossible despite long years of feuds, blood, faction, strife, hatreds, and deep-rooted animosity.

The answer is not difficult, nor is it impossible, if we sincerely and faithfully follow a straight line.

You want to live with us, part of the world.

In all sincerity I tell you we welcome you among us with full security and safety. This in itself is a tremendous turning point, one of the landmarks of a decisive historical change. We used to reject you. We had our reasons and our fears, yes.

We refused to meet with you, anywhere, yes.

We were together in international conferences and organizations, and our representatives did not, and still do not, exchange greetings with you. Yes. This has happened and is still happening.

It is also true that we used to set as a precondition for any negotiations with you a mediator who would meet separately with each party.

Yes. Through this procedure, the talks of the first and second disengagement agreements took place.

camouflage   hide

Our delegates met in the first Geneva conference without exchanging a direct word. Yes, this has happened.

Yet today I tell you, and I declare it to the whole world, that we accept to live with you in permanent peace based on justice. We do not want to encircle you or be encircled ourselves by destructive missiles ready for launching, nor by the shells of grudges and hatreds. . . .

I hail the Israeli voices that call for the recognition of the Palestinian people's right to achieve and safeguard peace.

Here I tell you, ladies and gentlemen, that it is no use to refrain from recognizing the Palestinian people and their right to statehood as their right of return. We, the Arabs, have faced this experience before, with you. And with the reality of the Israeli existence, the struggle which took us from war to war, from victims to more victims, until you and we have today reached the edge of a horrible abyss and a terrifying disaster unless, together, we seize this opportunity today of a durable peace based on justice.

You have to face reality bravely, as I have done. There can never be a solution to a problem by evading it or turning a deaf ear to it. Peace cannot last if attempts are made to impose fantasy concepts on which the world has turned its back and announced its unanimous call for the respect of rights and facts.

There is no need to enter a vicious circle as to Palestinian rights. It is useless to create obstacles; otherwise, the march of peace will be impeded or peace will be blown up. As I have told you, there is no happiness based on the detriment of others.

Direct confrontation and straightforwardness are the shortcuts and the most successful way to reach a clear objective. Direct confrontation concerning the Palestinian problem and tackling it in one single language with a view to achieving a durable and just peace lie in the establishment of that peace. With all the guarantees you demand,

there should be no fear of a newly born state that needs the assistance of all countries of the world.

When the bells of peace ring, there will be no hands to beat the drums of war. Even if they existed, they would be stilled. . . .

Ladies and gentlemen, peace is not a mere endorsement of written lines. Rather, it is a rewriting of history. Peace is not a game of calling for peace to defend certain whims or hide certain admissions. Peace in its essence is a dire struggle against all and every ambition and whim.

Perhaps the example taken and experienced, taken from ancient and modern history, teaches that missiles, warships, and nuclear weapons cannot establish security. Instead, they destroy what peace and security build.

For the sake of our peoples and for the sake of the civilization made by man, we have to defend man everywhere against rule by the force of arms so that we may endow the full of humanity with all the power of the values and principles that further the sublime position of mankind.

Allow me to address my call from this rostrum to the people of Israel. I tell them, from the Egyptian people, who bless this sacred mission of peace, I convey to you the message of peace of the Egyptian people, who do not harbor fanaticism and whose sons—Moslems, Christians and Jews—live together in a state of cordiality, love, and tolerance.

This is Egypt, whose people have entrusted me with their sacred message. A message of security, safety, and peace to every man, woman, and child in Israel. Let all endeavors be channeled toward building a huge stronghold for peace instead of building destructive rockets.

Introduce to the entire world the image of the new man in this area so that he might set an example to the man of our age, the man of peace everywhere. Ring the bells for

---

rostrum platform upon which a speaker stands
fanaticism very extreme beliefs that sometimes lead
  to violent behavior

cordiality politeness
endeavor effort

your sons. Tell them that those wars were the last of wars and the end of sorrows. Tell them that we are entering upon a new beginning, a new life, a life of love, prosperity, freedom, and peace.

You, sorrowing mother, you, widowed wife, you, the son who lost a brother or a father, all the victims of wars, fill the air and space with recitals of peace, fill bosoms and hearts with the aspirations of peace. Make a reality that blossoms and lives. Make hope a code of conduct and endeavor.

The will of peoples is part of the will of God. Ladies and gentlemen, before I came to this place, with every beat of my heart and with every sentiment, I prayed to God Almighty. While performing the prayers at the Al Aksa mosque and while visiting the Holy Sepulcher I asked the Almighty to give me strength and to confirm my belief that this visit may achieve the objective I look forward to for a happy present and a happier future.

I have chosen to set aside all precedents and traditions known by warring countries. In spite of the fact that occupation of Arab territories is still there, the declaration of my readiness to proceed to Israel came as a great surprise that stirred many feelings and confounded many minds. Some of them even doubted its intent.

Despite all that, the decision was inspired by all the clarity and purity of belief and with all the true passions of my people's will and intentions, and I have chosen this road considered by many to be the most difficult road.

I have chosen to come to you with an open heart and an open mind. I have chosen to give this great impetus to all international efforts exerted for peace. I have chosen to present to you, in your own home, the realities, devoid of any scheme or whim. Not to maneuver, or win a round, but for us to win together the most dangerous of rounds embattled in modern history, the battle of permanent peace based on justice.

It is not my battle alone. Nor is it the battle of the leadership in Israel alone. It is the battle of all and every citizen in our territories, whose right it is to live in peace. It is the commitment of conscience and responsibility in the hearts of millions.

When I put forward this initiative, many asked what is it that I conceived as possible to achieve during this visit and what my expectations were. And as I answer the questions, I announce before you that I have not thought of carrying out this initiative from the precepts of what could be achieved during this visit. And I have come here to deliver a message. I have delivered the message, and may God be my witness.

I repeat with Zachariah: Love, right, and justice. From the holy Koran I quote the following verses: We believe in God and in what has been revealed to us and what was revealed to Abraham, Ishmael, Isaac, Jacob, and the thirteen Jewish tribes. And in the books given to Moses and Jesus and the prophets from their Lord, who made no distinction between them. So we agree. *Salam Aleikum*—Peace be upon you.

mosque   Muslim house of worship
precedent   action or choice that creates expectations for future behavior
confounded   confused
impetus   push to get started
initiative   plan of action
precept   assumption

Zachariah, and so on   Sadat is referring to figures from the Jewish and Christian bibles and from the Muslim holy book, the Koran.
Salam Aleikum   an Arabic phrase similar to the Hebrew phrase Shalom Aleichem, which means "Peace be with you"

Think It Over

1. Do you think President el-Sadat made the right decision to speak to the Israeli Knesset? Why or why not?

2. Why do you think President el-Sadat referred to people and words that are holy to Jews, Christians, and Muslims?

SUDAN

from "A Handful of Dates"
by Tayeb Salih, translated by Denys Johnson-Davies

The author of this story is from Sudan, in North Africa. Most people living in this part of Africa are Muslims, or followers of the religion Islam. The holy book of Muslims is called the Quran, spelled by the translator of this story Koran. Understanding and following the Quran's teachings is a central part of Muslim life. Muslims pray five times each day. In this story, a young boy helps his grandfather complete this ritual.

I must have been very young at the time. While I don't remember exactly how old I was, I do remember that when people saw me with my grandfather they would pat me on the head and give my cheek a pinch— things they didn't do to my grandfather. The strange thing was that I never used to go out with my father, rather it was my grandfather who would take me with him wherever he went, except for the mornings when I would go to the mosque to learn the Koran. The mosque, the river and the fields—these were the landmarks in our life. While most of the children of my age grumbled at having to go to the mosque to learn the Koran, I used to love it. The reason was, no doubt, that I was quick at learning by heart and the Sheikh always asked me to stand up and recite the *Chapter of the Merciful* whenever we had visitors, who would pat me on my head and cheek just as people did when they saw me with my grandfather.

Yes, I used to love the mosque, and I loved the river too. Directly we finished our Koran reading in the morning I would throw down my wooden slate and dart off, quick as a genie, to my mother, hurriedly swallow down my breakfast, and run off for a plunge in the river. When tired of swimming about I would sit on the bank and gaze at the strip of water that wound away eastwards and hid behind a thick wood of acacia trees. I loved to give rein to my imagination and picture to myself a tribe of giants living behind that wood, a people tall and thin with white beards and sharp noses, like my grandfather. Before my grandfather ever replied to my many questions he would rub the tip of his nose with his forefinger; as for his beard, it was soft and luxuriant and as white as cotton-wool—never in my life have I seen anything of a purer whiteness or greater beauty. My grandfather must also have been extremely tall, for I never saw anyone in the whole area address him without having to look up at him, nor did I see him enter a house without having to bend so low that I was put in mind of the way the river wound round behind the wood of acacia trees. I loved him and would imagine myself, when I grew to be a man, tall and slender like him, walking along with great strides.

I believe I was his favourite grandchild: no wonder, for my cousins were a stupid bunch and I—so they say—was an intelligent child. I used to know when my grandfather wanted me to laugh, when to be silent; also I would remember the times for his prayers and would bring him his prayer-rug and fill the ewer for his ablutions without his having to ask me. When he had nothing else to do he enjoyed listening to me reciting to him from the Koran in a lilting voice, and I could tell from his face that he was moved.

mosque   Muslim house of worship
genie   magical spirit from Arab folklore
luxuriant   growing in great abundance

ewer   a wide-mouthed pitcher for holding water
ablutions   a washing of the body, especially before prayer

Think It Over

1. What role did religion play in the lives of the boy and his grandfather?

2. How did their feeling for the Quran bring the boy and his grandfather close?

CONGO

Interview With Congolese Villagers, 1893

from *Africa: The Struggle for Independence* by Dennis Wepman

The Congo Free State was one of the first African areas colonized. It was taken by Belgium during the rule of King Leopold. It is now the independent nation of Zaire. Here, Congolese villagers describe conditions under colonial rule.

From our country each village had to take 20 loads of rubber. . . . We had to take these loads in four times a month. . . . We got no pay. We got nothing. . . . Our village got cloth and a little salt, but not the people who did the work. . . . It used to take 10 days to get the 20 baskets of rubber—we were always in the forest to find the rubber vines, to go without food, and our women had to give up cultivating the fields and gardens. Then we starved. Wild beasts—the leopards—killed some of us while we were working away in the forest and others got lost or died from exposure or starvation and we begged the white men to leave us alone, saying we could get no more rubber, but the white men and their soldiers said: Go. You are only beasts yourselves. You are only Nyama [meat]. We tried, always going further into the forest,

and when we failed and our rubber was short, the soldiers came to our towns and killed us. Many were shot, some had their ears cut off; others were tied up with ropes around their necks and bodies and taken away. . . .

We used to hunt elephants long ago and there were plenty in our forests, and we got much meat; but Bula Matari [the Congo state] killed the elephant hunters because they could not get rubber, and so we starved. We are sent out to get rubber, and when we come back with little rubber we are shot. . . . [S]ometimes we brought rubber into the white man's stations. . . . when it was not enough the white man would put some of us in lines, one behind the other, and would shoot us through all our bodies.

cultivating   preparing land for use in growing crops
exposure   illness caused by lack of protection from heat, sun, and other elements of nature

Name _____ Date _____

GHANA
"Ghanian Leader Speaks Out"
from *Africa: The Struggle for Independence* by Dennis Wepman

Ghana, which was once called the Gold Coast, won its independence from Great Britain in 1957. As head of the new nation's government, President Kwame Nkrumah was the first African to lead a black government since colonial rule began. In 1961, he spoke to representatives of the United Nations.

Over 200 million of our people cry out with one voice of tremendous power—and what do they say? We do not ask for death for our oppressors, we do not pronounce wishes of ill-fate for our slave masters, we make an assertion of a just and positive demand. Our voice booms across the oceans and mountains, it calls for freedom for Africa. Africa wants her freedom. Africa must be free. . . .

For years Africa has been the footstool of colonialism and imperialism, exploitation and degradation. . . . Her sons languished in the chains of slavery and humiliation, and African exploiters and self-appointed controllers of her destiny strode across her land with incredible inhumanity, without mercy, without shame, without honour. These days are gone for ever and now I, an African, stand before this august Assembly of the United Nations and shall speak with the voice of freedom proclaiming to the world the dawn of a new era.

oppressors   those who control with unfair force
assertion   claim or demand
imperialism   the policy of extending one nation's power to control other nations

exploitation   unfair use for selfish reasons
degradation   the process of change from a positive state to a negative state
languished   grew weak and feeble

Eyewitness Account ★★★★★★

SOUTH AFRICA
The Words of Desmond Tutu
from *Desmond Tutu* by David Winner

During the 1980's, South African Archbishop Desmond Tutu spoke out often against apartheid. He worked to bring black and white South Africans toward a common goal—the peaceful end of apartheid.

"Don't delay our freedom, which is your freedom as well, for freedom is indivisible."
—*Desmond Tutu,*
in Hope and Suffering

"How do we compute the cost [of apartheid] in the legacy of bitterness, anger, frustration and indeed hatred which we are leaving behind for our children?"
—*Desmond Tutu,*
in Hope and Suffering

"You are told by those who are powerful . . . that you must move from your property because they want it. . . . Your community is being destroyed. You are being asked to abandon your South African citizenship. . . . It is almost as if you are being stoned to death as a community. . . ."
—*Desmond Tutu, to a*
group of black villagers

"I want to make this correspondence available to the press . . . so that all our people, both Black and White, will know that from our side we have done all that it is humanly possible to do, to appeal, not only to the rank and file of Whites, but to the highest political figure in the land, and to have issued the grave warning contained in my letter. This flows from a deep love and anguish for my country."
—*Desmond Tutu, in his letter to*
Prime Minister John Vorster

"My vision is of a South Africa that is totally nonracial. It will be a society that is more just. . . . Freedom is indivisible. Whites can't enjoy their separate freedoms. They spend too much time and resources defending those freedoms instead of enjoying them."
—*Desmond Tutu,*
in Hope and Suffering

"To be impartial . . . is indeed to have taken sides already . . . with the status quo."
—*Desmond Tutu,*
in Hope and Suffering

"Blacks don't want crumbs of concessions from the master's table. They want to be there determining the menu together."
—*Desmond Tutu,*
in Hope and Suffering

"Blacks are exceedingly patient and peace-loving. We are aware that politics is the art of the possible."
—*Desmond Tutu, in his letter to*
Prime Minister John Vorster

"We need one another, and Blacks have tried to assure Whites that they don't want to drive them into the sea. How long can they go on giving these assurances and have them thrown back in their faces with contempt?"
—*Desmond Tutu, in his letter to*
Prime Minister John Vorster

---

indivisible   cannot be divided
legacy   something handed down from one generation to another
nonracial   without concern for the race of the citizens
impartial   not favoring one more than the other
status quo   the present state of affairs

concession   right given in bargaining just to keep the other side happy
assurance   promise meant to give comfort and relieve worry
contempt   scorn; the attitude that a person or an idea is worthless

Think It Over

1. What do you think might have eventually happened to the rubber harvest in the Congo Free State?

2. What did Kwame Nkrumah ask for in his speech? Why are many black Africans so angry with their former European colonists?

3. Which historical speaker for Africa did you find most inspiring? Why?

WEST AFRICA

The Royal Kingdoms of Ghana, Mali, and Songhay
by Patricia and Frederick McKissack

In these selections, three observers from long ago describe the medieval African empires in Ghana, Mali, and Songhay. These West African empires thrived between A.D. 1000 and A.D. 1500 and made their success through trade.

Al-Bakri was an 11th century nobleman living in Spain. He gathered information from written sources and interviewed people who had visited Ghana before writing his description of the court. Ibn Battuta was a Moroccan Berber who made a journey to Mecca as part of his Islamic religion. His travels in the mid-1300's brought him to the Malian empire. Leo Africanus was forced to leave Spain in the late 1400's with all Muslims. Living in Africa, he traveled throughout the Sudan and visited Songhay's city of Timbuktu.

Al-Bakri Describes the Court of Ghana

When [the king] gives audience to the people, to listen to their complaints and set them to rights, he sits in a pavilion around which stand his horses caparisoned in cloth of gold; behind him stand ten pages holding shields and gold-mounted swords; and on his right hand are the sons of the princes of his empire, splendidly clad and with gold plaited into their hair. The governor of the city is seated on the ground in front of the king, and all around him are his viziers in the same position. The gate of the chamber is guarded by dogs of an excellent breed, who never leave the king's seat; they wear collars of gold and silver.

Ibn Battuta Praises the Fairness of Mali's People

The Highest Compliment

During his travels in the Malian empire, Ibn Battuta wrote about his observations of the people, their ruler, their customs and beliefs. He gave one of the highest compliments to a nation of people about justice:

Of all peoples the Negroes are those who most abhor injustice. The Sultan pardons no one who is guilty of it. There is complete and general safety throughout the land. The traveler here has no more reason than the man who stays at home to fear brigands, thieves or ravishers. . . . The blacks do not confiscate the goods of any North Africans who may die in their country, not even when these consist of large treasures. On the contrary, they deposit these goods with a man of confidence . . . until those who have a right to the goods present themselves and take possession.

Short on Hospitality

While visiting Mali's capital, Ibn Battuta was received by the king, who was at that time Mansa Musa's son. Ibn Battuta was offended by the king's lack of generosity. The traveler complained that the king was miserly and instead of giving him "robes of honor and money," he offered Ibn Battuta. . . three cakes of bread, a piece of beef fried in native oil, and a calabash of sour curds.

caparisoned covered in a decorative cloth
plaited braided
vizier a high official of the government
abhor hate

brigand bandit, outlaw
ravisher kidnapper
confiscate to seize by authority

Leo Africanus Describes Timbuktu

In 1510, Leo's uncle made the cross-Saharan trip via Sijilmasa-Taghaza to Timbuktu. Leo traveled with him and later wrote about his adventures.

. . . of Timbuktu

"Here are many shops of artificers and merchants, and especially of such as weave linnen [sic] and cotton cloth. And hither do the Barbary merchants bring cloth of Europe. All the women of this region except the maid servants go with their faces covered, and sell all necessary victuals. The inhabitants, and especially strangers living there, are exceeding rich, insomuch that the king married both his daughters unto two rich merchants. Here are many wells containing most sweet water; and so often as the River Niger overflowth they convey the water thereof by sluices into the town. Corn, cattle, milk, and butter this region yields in great abundance: but salt is very scarce here, for it is brought hither by land from Taghaza. . . ."

. . . of Gao

Leo wrote: "It is a wonder to see what plenty of merchandise is daily brought hither, and how costly and sumptuous all things be. Horses bought in Europe for ten ducats are sold again for forty and sometimes for fifty ducats apiece. There is not any cloth of Europe so coarse, which will not here be sold for four ducats an ell and if it be anything fine they will give fifteen ducats for an ell; and an ell of the scarlet of Venice or of Turkey-cloth is here worth thirty ducats. A sword is here valued at three or four crowns and so likewise are spurs, bridles, with other like commodities, and spices also are sold at a high rate: but of all other commodities salt is most extremely dear."

artificers craftspeople
linnen linen, a fabric
hither here

victuals foods, supplies
sluice a gate for controlling the flow of water

Think It Over

1. Describe one feature of each kingdom.

2. How were the kingdoms of Mali, Ghana, and Songhay similar? How were they different?

UGANDA

from *Mukasa*
by John Nagenda

Mukasa lived in a small Ugandan village in the 1940's. For a long time, he did not go to school. Finally, his family gathered enough money to pay his school fees by working extra and asking relatives for help. When the first day of school arrived, Mukasa was a little bit afraid.

At last the day arrived. By five in the morning Mukasa was awake. It had been a difficult night for sleep, strung out with dreams. He looked outside and it was still completely dark, but he knew that he could not go back to sleep. Then gradually objects started looming up around him as if a breath of lighter darkness was sweeping over them. Slowly the morning filled out, until the coming sun covered the eastern sky like a dye. All this Mukasa watched, and heard the first crying of the birds and the croaking of the frogs, and felt with some sadness that something of him was disappearing with the darkness.

The previous evening it was as if Mukasa were going on a long journey. His mother cooked the kind of food only prepared for the most important occasions. There was chicken and beef and spinach and rice and plantain and cassava and sweet potatoes and beans and groundnut sauce.

His grandfather said, "Mukasa, you should start school every day. Why this is better than Christmas! Pass me some of that chicken!"

Whether you were a Christian or not, Christmas was a great excuse for feasting!

And even Mukasa's father seemed to be enjoying himself.

The two men sat at a small table, with the women and Mukasa on the ground below them.

"Have some more, our learned one," said his grandmother, laughing, and heaping food on Mukasa's plate. "By tomorrow morning it'll be too late."

His mother said, "Watch that stomach. We don't want you sick tomorrow!"

But she too kept giving him more food.

When they could not eat any more, his father belched and said, "Well, it's only right I should make a little speech."

Out of the corner of his eye Mukasa looked at his mother. She was looking at his father.

"Let no one say it was my idea for Mukasa to go to school," his father said. "What I think about it, we all know. In my day children stayed at home with their parents and helped them. As for giving you any advice on your new life, my boy, I of course know nothing about it, being a village fool. Your teachers will do that, and I hear their canes are very good at it."

"Now, now, my fellow man," said the grandfather, "there is no reason to frighten the boy. We don't know what'll happen to him, but for myself I wish him luck, and if he is my grandson he'll do all right."

He reached out his hand and pulled Mukasa up to him. He looked at Mukasa and smiled, the kind of smile he had when he told him stories. His grandfather's eyes were very old and his face was full of lines, but when he smiled like this it was like a boy smiling.

"Show your father, boy," his grandfather had said loudly.

Now at six in the morning his mother called out to tell him to get up and start getting ready. Soon she came and took him off to wash him, although for more than a year now he had washed himself. The cold water made him shiver until he could not talk. His mother stood over him, the smell of the soap

plantain a kind of banana
cassava an edible root plant
groundnut an edible root plant

learned educated
cane stick used for striking children who broke the rules

was in his nostrils, the cold water seemed to reach into every corner of his body. The bright color of the sun was still without warmth, and in the cold of early morning the plantain gardens looked greener than they would at noon, and within them it was still surprisingly dark.

By the time some warmth had returned to his stomach and his shivering had subsided, there was just enough time for Mukasa to have a quick bite: a warmed-up chunk of last night's plantain meal, washed down by a cup of weak tea without milk. Not that he had any appetite.

Then his mother helped him on with his new uniform. The shorts were too big and so was the shirt. It was the first time he had worn the uniform outside the shop where it had been made, and its smell reminded him of the shop: but above all it had the smell of khaki cloth which is new and hasn't been washed. Mukasa loved it.

His legs and arms looked a little rough and chapped and his mother rubbed some soap over them till they gleamed. Down in the valley where the school was, the first drum was sounding.

One of Namata's boys had told him the day before that the first drum always sounded half an hour before the second, and after the second you only had five minutes before you were late. If you were late you were lined up with others like yourself and you were in trouble.

It was time to go. He had a small bag with a book, a pencil, an eraser and a ruler in it. Now his mother gave him the money for his school fees and he put it in the bag. The money was in a used envelope and you would not have guessed that in this small envelope was the result of so much effort.

Even as he put the envelope away, Mukasa remembered the endless journeys he and his mother had made for the money. Sometimes his mother went alone, sometimes they went together. And on one of the journeys he had had his first ride in a motor vehicle, the old, old bus that coughed its way

through the village once a week. It had taken Mukasa and his mother to a small town twenty miles away where a distant relative lived. Mukasa had never even imagined such a big place before.

Slowly the money had been collected, until there was enough for the first term or two at school. Mukasa sometimes wondered whether some of his relatives, in spite of their kindness, considered him and his mother something of a nuisance.

Meanwhile they had started the cotton plot to supplement what money they received. It seemed to Mukasa that he knew every plant, and he remembered the thrill with which he had seen the dug-up soil waiting for the seed. All this is for me and my going to school, he had thought. The thrill was repeated when the plants came up, and when the buds grew. Now some of them were beginning to burst into the white cotton, and soon it would be ready for picking.

Mukasa's house faced the road to the school. He had watched the schoolchildren going down the road and at times they seemed like a river of yelling khaki. It started in a trickle, one or two individuals walking at leisure, and ended again in a trickle, a swift one now. But the middle of it seemed fit to burst, and this first morning he intended to be ahead of it.

He wondered whether his father was awake to hear him go. He said a last good-by to his mother and was off, pretending a confidence that he didn't feel. He turned round once to wave to his mother and saw her standing beside their house, a small shadow beside the shadow of the house, with the sun full behind. And then at the road he broke into a trot, although it was still early. The strings of his bag were around his neck, leaving his hands free. And the bag itself hit him now on the right thigh and now on the left as he ran down toward the valley.

Everything seemed somehow different this morning: the road, the color of the hills, even the brightness of the morning light.

subsided lessened

supplement add to

He came round the final corner and saw the buildings of the school half a mile away below him, with a few tiny figures already dotted about them. He started to feel his heart pound with excitement, in addition to all his nervousness, for quite soon he would be part of the school, and there was no way yet of knowing what would happen.

Think It Over

1. How do you think Mukasa and his family felt about him going to school?

2. What did Mukasa and his mother have to do to get the money for his schooling? Why was this probably hard for them?

INDIA

A Great Asian Thinker

from *The Dhammapada*, translated by Eknath Easwaran

In the 400's and 500's B.C., Siddhartha Gautama lived near the present-day border of India and Nepal. Gautama had been born a prince but felt it was wrong to live such a comfortable life when so many people were suffering. He searched for answers. He was later called the Buddha, or "enlightened one," because he reached a new level of spiritual understanding. Buddha's ideas remain an important influence in Asia and other parts of the world.

More than those who hate you, more than all your enemies, an undisciplined mind does greater harm. More than your mother, more than your father, more than all your family, a well-disciplined mind does greater good.

Do not give your attention to what others do or fail to do; give it to what you do or fail to do.

Like a lovely flower, full of color but lacking in fragrance, are the words of those who do not practice what they preach. Like a lovely flower full of color and fragrance are the words of those who practice what they preach.

Many garlands can be made from a heap of flowers. Many good deeds can be done in this life.

The immature are their own enemies, doing selfish deeds which will bring them sorrow. That deed is selfish which brings remorse and suffering in its wake. But good is that deed which brings no remorse, only happiness in its wake.

If you see a wise man who steers you away from the wrong path, follow him as you would one who can reveal hidden treasures. Only good can come out of it.

Make friends with those who are good and true, not with those who are bad and false.

As irrigators lead water where they want, as archers make their arrows straight, as carpenters carve wood, the wise shape their minds.

garland   wreath

Think It Over

1. Based on these quotations, what ideas did Buddha believe in most strongly?

2. How are the ideas of Buddha similar and different from those of other great thinkers you have studied?

INDIA
"Savitri: A Tale of Ancient India"
retold by Aaron Shepard

The Hindu religion of India has a rich tradition of ancient legends. Many, like the tale of Savitri, include Hindu gods among their characters. This story is a favorite among the Hindu people. It is unusual for this region because its main character is a woman, Savitri. She is a princess named after a goddess. Her name is also the name of a prayer to the sun god. Princess Savitri's devotion, courage, and wisdom prove her to be a true hero.

In India, in the time of legend, there lived a king with many wives but not one child. Morning and evening for eighteen years, he faced the fire on the sacred altar and prayed for the gift of children.

Finally, a shining goddess rose from the flames.

"I am Savitri, child of the Sun. By your prayers, you have won a daughter."

Within a year, a daughter came to the king and his favorite wife. He named her Savitri, after the goddess.

Beauty and intelligence were the princess Savitri's, and eyes that shone like the sun. So splendid was she, people thought she herself was a goddess. Yet, when the time came for her to marry, no man asked for her.

Her father told her, "Weak men turn away from radiance like yours. Go out and find a man worthy of you. Then I will arrange the marriage."

In the company of servants and councilors, Savitri traveled from place to place. After many days, she came upon a hermitage by a river crossing. Here lived many who had left the towns and cities for a life of prayer and study.

Savitri entered the hall of worship and bowed to the eldest teacher. As they spoke, a young man with shining eyes came into the hall. He guided another man, old and blind.

"Who is that young man?" asked Savitri softly.

"That is Prince Satyavan," said the teacher, with a smile. "He guides his father, a king whose realm was conquered. It is well that Satyavan's name means 'Son of Truth,' for no man is richer in virtue."

When Savitri returned home, she found her father sitting with the holy seer named Narada.

"Daughter," said the king, "have you found a man you wish to marry?"

"Yes, Father," said Savitri. "His name is Satyavan."

Narada gasped. "Not Satyavan! Princess, no man could be more worthy, but you must not marry him! I know the future. Satyavan will die, one year from today."

The king said, "Do you hear, Daughter? Choose a different husband!"

Savitri trembled but said, "I have chosen Satyavan, and I will not choose another. However long or short his life, I wish to share it."

Soon the king rode with Savitri to arrange the marriage.

Satyavan was overjoyed to be offered such a bride. But his father, the blind king, asked Savitri, "Can you bear the hard life of the hermitage? Will you wear our simple robe and our coat of matted bark? Will you eat only fruit and plants of the wild?"

Savitri said, "I care nothing about comfort or hardship. In palace or in hermitage, I am content."

That very day, Savitri and Satyavan walked hand in hand around the sacred fire in the hall of worship.

In front of all the priests and hermits, they became husband and wife.

sacred altar   place of worship
radiance   glow
seer   holy person who has the ability to know future events

hermits   people who live in a hermitage, or secluded place of prayer

For a year, they lived happily. But Savitri could never forget that Satyavan's death drew closer. Finally, only three days remained. Savitri entered the hall of worship and faced the sacred fire. There she prayed for three days and nights, not eating or sleeping.

"My love," said Satyavan, "prayer and fasting are good. But why be this hard on yourself?"

Savitri gave no answer.

The sun was just rising when Savitri at last left the hall. She saw Satyavan heading for the forest, an ax on his shoulder.

Savitri rushed to his side. "I will come with you."

"Stay here, my love," said Satyavan. "You should eat and rest."

But Savitri said, "My heart is set on going."

Hand in hand, Savitri and Satyavan walked over wooded hills. They smelled the blossoms on flowering trees and paused beside clear streams. The cries of peacocks echoed through the woods.

While Savitri rested, Satyavan chopped firewood from a fallen tree. Suddenly, he dropped his ax.

"My head aches," he said.

Savitri rushed to him. She laid him down in the shade of a tree, his head on her lap.

"My body is burning!" said Satyavan. "What is wrong with me?"

Satyavan's eyes closed. His breathing slowed.

Savitri looked up. Coming through the woods to meet them was a princely man. He shone, though his skin was darker than the darkest night. His eyes and his robe were the red of blood.

Trembling, Savitri asked, "Who are you?"

A deep, gentle voice replied. "Princess, you see me only by the power of your prayer and fasting. I am Yama, god of death. Now is the time I must take the spirit of Satyavan."

Yama took a small noose and passed it through Satyavan's breast, as if through air. He drew out a tiny likeness of Satyavan, no bigger than a thumb.

Satyavan's breathing stopped.

Yama placed the likeness inside his robe. "Happiness awaits your husband in my kingdom. Satyavan is a man of great virtue."

Then Yama turned and headed south, back to his domain.

Savitri rose and started after him.

Yama strode smoothly and swiftly through the woods, while Savitri struggled to keep up. At last, he stopped to face her.

"Savitri! You cannot follow to the land of the dead!"

"Lord Yama," said Savitri, "I know your duty is to take my husband. But my duty as his wife is to stay beside him."

"Princess, that duty is at an end," said Yama. "Still, I admire your loyalty. I will grant you a favor—anything but the life of your husband."

Savitri said, "Please restore my father-in-law's kingdom and his sight."

"His sight and his kingdom shall be restored."

Yama again headed south. Savitri followed.

Along a riverbank, thorns and tall sharp grass let Yama pass untouched. But they tore at Savitri's clothes and skin.

"Savitri! You have come far enough!"

"Lord Yama, I know my husband will find happiness in your kingdom. But you carry away the happiness that is mine!"

"Princess, even love must bend to fate," said Yama. "Still, I admire your devotion. I will grant you another favor—anything but the life of your husband."

Savitri said, "Grant many more children to my father."

"Your father shall have many more children."

Yama once more turned south. Again, Savitri followed.

Up a steep hill Yama glided, while Savitri clambered after him. At the top, he halted.

"Savitri! I forbid you to come farther!"

"Lord Yama, you are respected and revered by all. Yet, no matter what may come, I will remain by Satyavan!"

"Princess, I tell you for the last time, you will not!" said Yama. "Still, I can only admire your courage and your firmness. I will grant you one last favor—anything but the life of your husband."

"Then grant many children to *me*," said Savitri. "And let them be children of Satyavan!"

Yama's eyes grew wide as he stared at Savitri. "You did not ask for your husband's life, yet I cannot grant your wish without releasing him. Princess, your wit is as strong as your will."

Yama took out the spirit of Satyavan and removed the noose. The spirit flew north, quickly vanishing from sight.

"Return, Savitri. You have won your husband's life."

The sun was just setting when Savitri again laid Satyavan's head in her lap.

His chest rose and fell. His eyes opened. "Is the day already gone? I have slept long," he said. "But what is wrong, my love? You smile and cry at the same time!"

"My love," said Savitri, "let us return home."

Yama was true to all he had promised. Savitri's father became father to many more. Satyavan's father regained both sight and kingdom.

In time, Satyavan became king, and Savitri his queen. They lived long and happily, blessed with many children. So they had no fear or tears when Yama came again to carry them to his kingdom.

Think It Over

1. Why do you think Savitri chose Prince Satyavan? What about him attracted her?

2. What message does this tale try to teach?

SOUTHEAST ASIA

"The Tale of a Frog"
by the Shan People of Southern Annam

People who work to protect nature know that all the living things in the world are connected and interdependent. This traditional poem from Annam, a region in what is now Vietnam, gives an example of this connection.

"Heron, heron, why are you so lean?"
"I am lean because the shrimp don't come upstream."
"Shrimp, shrimp, why don't you come upstream?"
"I don't come upstream because the grass grows too thick."
"Grass, grass, why do you grow so thick?"
"I grow so thick because the water buffalo doesn't eat me."
"Buffalo, buffalo, why don't you eat the grass?"
"I don't eat the grass because the stake won't let me go."
"Stake, stake, why don't you let the buffalo go?"
"I don't let the buffalo go because the herdboy neglects his work."
"Herdboy, herdboy, why do you neglect your work?"
"I neglect my work because my stomach is empty."
"Stomach, stomach, why are you empty?"
"I am empty because the rice isn't cooked."
"Rice, rice, why aren't you cooked?"
"I am not cooked because the firewood is wet."
"Firewood, firewood, why are you wet?"
"I am wet because the rain never stops falling."
"Rain, rain, why do you never stop falling?"
"I never stop falling because the frog scratches his back."
"Frog, frog, why do you scratch your back?"
"I scratch my back because my ancestors have always scratched their backs. Why shouldn't I scratch mine?"

heron a bird

Think It Over

1. What effect does the climate of Southern Annam have on all the living creatures in the poem? Explain how each cause becomes an effect and each effect a cause.

CHINA

from *City Kids in China*
by Peggy Thomson

Students in the Ya-li Middle School in Changsha, China, offer a glimpse of modern city life in China. They talk about the importance of bicycles in a country where there are few privately owned cars. They tell about the One and Only policy which pressures Chinese families to have only one child. And, like children everywhere, they respond with different moods to the seasons and climate.

Every morning at six fifty I walk to the school. In winter I walk quickly with my hands in my pockets. It's cold and the wind blows. I have on a lot of clothes and move my legs faster and faster. I don't have a mood to see what happens around me. But in spring, in fall, a warm wind blows me warm and I see around myself—the trees, the people. I walk slowly in summer or I will be too hot. I sing in a low voice. Always I see the buses run more slowly than I walk. With friends on the way to school I speak jokes. I think what I should do in the noon and in the evening after my homework. I think, will my mother let me watch television?

—*Fei "Eric" Mins*

The History of My Bike.

I have a beautiful bike. His name is Forever. His hometown is the Shanghai Bicycle Factory. He is painted with black. He looks like a black treasure. Also some of him is bright, just like a mirror. When he is in the sun, he is dazzling.

The bike is a gift from my uncle. When he knew that I became a student of Ya-li Middle School, he gave the new bike to me as a present. How happy I am, because school is not near to my home and I hate to take the bus.

I often ride very fast because I get up late. One bad day I'm not in luck. My key is lost and I must take five minutes to look for it. After that I want my bike to go in the shortest time. But to my surprise the bike looks sick. He can't go quickly. He can't go even as

quickly as an old slow bus. So I am late and the teacher orders me to clean the classroom.

Sometimes I repair my bike myself. But I'm a not very good repairman. He becomes worse and worse. So I have to call my father for help. Sometimes also I'm a not careful rider. One day riding home, I saw a beautiful . . . car. I looked at it for a long time. And, *Ping!* I hit a . . . truck and fell to the ground. I picked up the bike very quickly because I saw a man come towards me. I rode very quickly and heard: Hi! Stop the child! I was not to pay attention to him, and I tried my best to get home. I was very satisfied with my speed. It was not the bike's fault—my fall—but a mistake I made.

Now I have ridden my bike for two years. He became older and not as beautiful as when he was new. But I still like him because he is one of my best friends.

—*Ming "Benjamin" Luo*

(NOTE: Chinese don't use words for 'he," "she," "it,"; hence they are apt to say in English "My brother, she is busy," and Benjamin says "My bike, he is beautiful.")

If you want to ride on a bus, you must have a big power. People stand with no room between. You must sway, like fish. If on the way you fall, the other persons must land on top of you.

—*Man "Laura" Luo*

I'm an only son. In school I feel lonely. My parents are often on a business trip. If I have a brother I can tell stories to him. I'll crack a joke to him. I'll tell him how to play chess. I'll teach him to play ball. I'll study with him and help him. When he's ten, I'll give him a bike of mine. After that we'll ride bikes to school. A brother can make fun. He can make me confident to do well in my studies. I wish I had a brother.

—*Ren "Thomas" Liu*

Think It Over

1. How does the weather affect Fei "Eric" Ming's mood and behavior?

2. Why do you think Ming "Benjamin" Luo has such a special relationship with his bicycle?

3. Why do you think Ren "Thomas" Liu wants to share these experiences with his imaginary brother?

SOUTH KOREA

from *The Year of Impossible Goodbyes*
by Sook Nyul Khoi

After World War II, the United States and the Soviet Union divided up the world into parts each would try to influence. Korea was divided into a communist North and a democratic South. Many North Koreans, unhappy with this situation, tried to escape to the South. In this story, ten-year-old Sookan and her younger brother Inchun have reached the final moments of their escape attempt and hope to be reunited with their family in South Korea.

We kept walking and finally reached the tracks, which would be our bridge to the South. The railroad ties of the tracks were made of wood and were spaced several feet apart. A grown-up would just be able to make it from one tie to the next. If we made one false move, we would fall into the rapidly flowing river, and would surely die. We looked in terror at the task ahead of us. Gripped with fear, we looked around. Now we could clearly see the barbed-wire fence and the well-lit tents ahead.

"*Nuna,* the old man said nothing about a river and railroad tracks. We must be in the wrong place."

"Look," I said, "that is the South. We have to cross this river by going over these cross-rungs. Then we can run to the fence. The sky is lighter now and we can see better. Mother might be there waiting for us. I don't know if this is the right place, but I don't see another way."

Inchun stared at the railroad ties and cried. "Mommy, Mommy," he kept sobbing.

We sat there for a long time staring at the long distance between the railroad ties and the river below. "Well, Inchun, I think we can do it. Get down on all fours and stretch out your arms one at a time and try to grab onto the next rung. I'll go first and we'll take each step slowly and carefully. Don't look down. Make sure you grab the wooden bar with your hands first, then move your legs one at a time. You can hold on to my ankles. I'll grab onto the next rung and tell you when

your hand and my ankle can move to the next one. Come on, there are the dogs and soldiers again." I had to reach out to grab the splintery rung, and my head started to spin when I looked at the dark turgid waters below. I was sure I would fall into the river, dragging Inchun with me.

Little Inchun looked at me and stretched his arms to reach the first rung. I turned and looked, and the gap between the rungs looked even larger than before; his little arms could barely reach. My whole body felt as if it were on fire. I was terribly afraid for him. He was brave. He said nothing, clenched his teeth with determination, and reached out to grab the rung and my ankle and carefully pull himself over. Rung by rung, we slowly continued. The light of dawn helped us to see the rungs. But the better we could see the path, the better the Russians would be able to see us. We kept crawling slowly from rung to rung until the land rose up beneath the tracks. We had crossed over the river and had about a quarter of a mile to go.

How inviting that barbed-wire fence seemed! Only that small distance separated us now. Mother might be waiting for us in one of those tents with the warm glowing lights. Inchun and I looked at each other and started running toward the fence. At any moment the Russian guards might spring upon us. It was misty and wet. We soon heard the fierce barking of dogs. They must have discovered our scent. We froze and stared at

barbed-wire   wire with sharp points sticking out along its length
cross-rungs   the pieces of wood or metal connecting the two long railroad tracks

railroad ties   another term for cross-rungs
turgid   swollen, moving fast

each other. The dogs were getting closer and closer and the barking grew louder and fiercer. We heard the soldiers' footsteps in the distance. We heard them shouting to one another.

It wasn't worth trying to hide anymore. It was now or never. We could see the fence right in front of us. We locked our hands together and ran as fast as we could. We just ran and ran, and finally reached the barbed-wire fence. Using all my remaining strength, I pulled at the bottom of the wire. It would not budge. There was no time to think. We fell to our knees and started to dig. We only made a tiny little space. Then I tried to lift the fence as much as I could. "Go, Inchun!" I urged. "Flatten yourself out like a snake and slide through, then keep running. I'll be right behind you."

Little Inchun slipped under the wire and then, instead of running as I had told him, he tried to lift the wire with his little hands. I heard the dogs drawing closer and I thrust my body under the wire. The barbs dug into me. My hair was caught, my clothes ripped, and I could feel the blood pooling in the cuts on my back. I kept going, and finally, I made it through. I grabbed Inchun's hand. We cried and kept running.

I did not look back to see how close the soldiers and the dogs were. I was too afraid. I could only look forward.

escapee   one who escapes

Inchun said, panting, "Are we in the South now?"

"Yes," I said, clutching his hand tighter.

"But I still hear the dogs and the soldiers," Inchun said.

"Don't worry, just run!" I squeezed his hand and pulled him forward. I had heard that once you were in the South, the Russians and the North Koreans could not shoot you, even if you were an escapee. But still we ran. They sounded as though they were right behind us. We kept running toward the lit tents. Then I saw four people rushing out of the tents and running to us. I saw the Red Cross sign on their white hats. They were carrying stretchers and medical bags, and I finally felt that we didn't have to run anymore.

I stopped and grabbed Inchun. "We can stop now," I told him. "We're safe, we're safe." My trembling legs collapsed under me and I fell to the ground. Inchun tumbled down on top of me. Exhaustion and relief overwhelmed us. I looked at him, and his eyes were closed. I felt dizzy and looked up at the sky, which was spinning above me. As I was lifted onto a stretcher, my eyes filled with tears. I heard the soothing voice of an older woman saying, "These poor children . . . all alone . . . Look at their feet. Hurry, let's get them inside. Hurry."

Think It Over

1. Why were Sookan and Inchun willing to take such risks to reach South Korea?

2. Do you think Sookan was a good older sister? Why or why not?

3. How do you think Sookan might feel in the years to come about the land she left behind? Why?

"The Coconut Tree"

from *Tales of the South Pacific Islands* by Anne Gittins

The cultures of the world have different ways of explaining natural features and behavior. This traditional tale from the South Pacific suggests one possible origin of the coconut tree, a resource for food and many other uses.

Long ago, in a faraway coral island set in the warm blue Pacific Ocean, there lived a beautiful maiden called Ina. She had raven-black hair and brown skin, and she lived with her parents in a house made of reeds with a thatched roof. Near her home there was a fresh-water stream in which there were always plenty of fish and large eels. It flowed swiftly over boulders and pebbles, and formed deep pools, and finally disappeared beneath the rocks.

Each day at dawn and sunset, Ina left her house and went to bathe in one of the pools near a clump of trees. One day a huge eel, larger than any she had ever seen, swam upstream from its hiding place beneath the rocks and startled her when she felt it touch her foot. But the eel did her no harm, and it returned so often that Ina became accustomed to seeing it and was no longer afraid of the creature.

One day as she watched it, to her great surprise the eel changed into a handsome young man.

"Do not be afraid of me," he said. "My name is Tuna, and I am the god and protector of all fresh-water eels. I have loved you for a long time, and I have now left the dark rocks where I live to try and win your love."

From that day he became her suitor. He changed into a young man whenever she came to visit him but turned into his old form of an eel when he returned to the stream.

There came a day when Tuna declared, "I must leave you now." But before he said good-bye to the maiden he told her that he would leave a wonderful gift so that she would always remember him.

"Tomorrow there will be a storm, and the rain will cause the stream to overflow and it will flood the valley. Do not be afraid, for I will swim up to your house on the hill, and when you see me in the form of an eel I will lay my head on your wooden doorstep. Cut off my head at once and bury it. Then go every day to look at the place, and wait and see what will happen."

Ina was very sad to think that she would see him no more, and she went slowly home. That night it rained and rained, and the noise on the roof was like thunder. She remembered what Tuna had said, and at dawn she looked outside and saw that the floods had indeed covered the valley and all its plantations and gardens, and that the water was just lapping the edge of her house. At that moment a large eel appeared. It swam right up to the entrance and laid its head on the doorstep. Ina ran and fetched her chopper made from a sharpened shell, and sadly she chopped off the eel's head. Then she buried it quickly on the hillside near her house.

After a while the rain ceased, and the waters drained away to a mere stream once more. Every day Ina visited the place where she had buried the head, but there was nothing to be seen. Then one day she found a tall green shoot growing, and each day it grew and grew and sent out long leaves.

By and by when it had become a tall tree, it flowered and bore fruit in the form of large

coral island   an island created when millions of tiny sea animals known as coral die and their skeletons pile up into rock-like formations
raven-black   a blueish black, the color of a raven bird

eel   a snakelike fish
accustomed   used to
suitor   one who hopes to win another's love
plantations   large farms

clusters of nuts. When they were husked Ina found that on each one were marks like Tuna's two eyes and mouth. He had kept his promise and left a gift in memory of his love for her. Her people also found that it was indeed a wonderful gift, for the tree had so many uses. The nuts gave them food and drink, and the leaves could be plaited by the villagers to make mats and fans and also sails for their canoes. With the leaves they thatched their houses, and as time went on they found many more uses for the trees that grew from those first nuts.

As time passed, it became the custom that whenever anyone went sailing from one island to another he would throw a nut into the sea. "Perhaps some starving shipwrecked man will need this nut," the traveler thought, "or perhaps it may grow upon some other island." And to this day the people of the Pacific still throw a coconut overboard whenever they travel by sea.

husked   the outer shell removed
thatched   covered the walls and/or roof with woven material

Think It Over

1. Why do you think Tuna left the coconut tree behind for Ina?

2. Why do you think it was so important to the people of the Cook Islands to have a story that explained the origins of the coconut tree?

3. What problems could occur in a culture that is very dependent on a single resource?

AUSTRALIA
"Family Council"
by Oodgeroo

A family is a small unit within a culture. The way people behave—make decisions, for example—shows something of what they expect from the world beyond their family. In this
memoir about her childhood on Stradbroke Island, Queensland, Australian Aborigine
Oodgeroo talks about how decisions were made within her family unit. Though she was
known to white Australians as Kath Walker, Oodgeroo returned in 1988 to her Aboriginal
name. It means "paperbark" and refers to the tree bark on which she wrote.

The family was holding one of its many council meetings. This time the grievance committee was airing its views. My two sisters and brothers were complaining that I did not pull my weight when it came to bringing home the food supplies from the hunt. They could all boast of a high tally of birds and animals they had brought home for the family larder. Although I always went hunting with them, I never did any good with my slingshot and bandicoot traps. They said I spent too much time dreaming, or gathering flowers, or looking for discarded feathers, or drawing trees and animals and birds in the sand. That never made any sense to them, because the water always came and washed away my efforts with the receding tide. If I wasn't doing these things, then they complained that I'd go tramping off through the bush.

They were right. I never did take home any birds or animals for the larder. However, I did try to make up for my bad hunting record in other ways.

My eldest brother was allowed to make the first complaint against me. "She shouldn't be allowed to eat the food we bring home," he said. "She goes barging into the swamps and clumps of bushes just when I get a line on an extra-choice fat bird—and then I miss it because my stupid sister has warned it of our presence."

My second brother said darkly, "I think she gets up early and beats us to the bandicoot traps to let the creatures out."

My elder sister chipped in now. "She won't even help to carry home the bandicoots or birds when we do catch them."

My younger sister was not to be left out. "She deliberately puts Spitfire into her bandicoot trap to chase away the bandicoots. That cat of hers is wild—just like her! None of us can get anywhere near Spitfire except for her. She has it trained to frighten us away."

When my father finally asked me to speak, I didn't have much to say. All I could answer was that although it was true I didn't catch any game, it was quite untrue that I ever deliberately barged in to chase it away. Sometimes I just forgot about the need to keep still and quiet. And though I had a habit of getting up earlier than the others, I never released the bandicoots out of the traps. As for my younger sister, she was talking through her hat. I always set my bandicoot trap in just the same way as everyone else, but each time I went to see if I'd caught a bandicoot in it, I always found my cat in the trap instead. And it was, in fact, Spitfire that my brother had seen me releasing from the trap one morning, not a bandicoot! I had nothing to say to answer my elder sister's complaint that I would not carry the dead birds and animals home. I simply told my father straight out that I didn't like to do that.

Father was our arbitration judge. The rules were simple. Either we agreed with his

grievance complaint
airing sharing
tally count
slingshot simple weapon for shooting stones
bandicoot large rat

discarded thrown away
larder food storage container
arbitration a method of settling disagreements in
    which a judge makes the final decision

decision, or we unanimously opposed it and appealed for another hearing. Having listened to the complaints and my defense, it was now his job to overrule the plaintiffs, if he could. I certainly hadn't been much help to him.

He turned to my brothers and sisters. "Who catches the most fish, and goes fishing most often of all of you?"

They had to admit that I was the best fisherman in the family.

"And who is best at crab spotting and catching?" my father went on.

Again they admitted that it was me.

"And the shellfish—how often is this gathered, and who spends the most time filling the bags with it?"

unanimously   all in agreement

Yes, they agreed that I did.

"So," said my father, "your sister has earned her place at the table. Even a fisherman must eat in order to fish."

There were never any more complaints against me after this. The others accepted the fact that they would have to put up with my bad hunting, and that I would never change. So I went on fishing, looking for crabs, and gathering shellfish—and I went on collecting fallen feathers, ferns and flowers while my brothers and sisters worked hard to bring home the rest of the game.

plaintiffs   those who bring a complaint

Think It Over

1. Does the process of arbitration in this story seem like a fair method for settling disagreements? Why or why not?

2. What character traits did Father value?

3. How does the decision-making process in this family compare to those you are familiar with?

AUSTRALIA

from *The Road From Coorain*
by Jill Ker Conway

The place we live helps shape our personality and expectations. For Jill Ker and her family, life on a sheep farm in New South Wales was very often a struggle for survival. In one period of drought, it didn't rain for eight years! Jill had to struggle to find friends as well. Neighbors were miles away and there was no telephone. Here she describes some of her family's earliest struggles and the wondrous changes rain brings to their lives.

They called the new property Coorain, an aboriginal word which means windy place. The house they built was of weatherboard, with the ubiquitous corrugated iron roof of bush houses. It was a low-spreading bungalow, surrounded by verandas on all sides to catch the cooling breezes of summer when the thermometer would settle in over 100 degrees for weeks at a time. My father's bush sense made him site the house out in the open blazing sun, because wherever there were trees for shelter was where the water gathered after heavy rain. Visitors mocked his decision and asked why he had not taken advantage of the shade offered by the low-lying clump of trees just behind the site of the house. He was proved wise when the next wet year came. Other houses were flooded, but Coorain was not.

They were desperately short of water. The only supply came from the rain which was collected on the broad, gently sloping roof of the house. Optimistically, they planted a line of sugar gums along the east, north, and south of the house, and to the west, fast-growing pepper trees which were drought resistant and would soon shade the house from the afternoon heat. Climbing vines were planted to shade the verandas and a few geraniums decorated small beds by the front entrance. It was extremely hard to grow anything when the only water to be had was bailed out of the bathtub after the children were bathed in the evening. There was water

deep underground, but it was costly to bore down to it, and the first investment had to be made in good water for sheep and cattle. So there was no garden, no fresh fruit or vegetables, and no way to mitigate the red baked soil, the flatness, and the loneliness.

In the next few weeks it continued to rain more, so that an unheard-of eight inches had fallen within less than a month. The transformation of the countryside was magical. As far as the eye could see wild flowers exploded into bloom. Each breeze would waft their pollen round the house, making it seem as though we lived in an enormous garden. Everywhere one looked the sites of old creek beds became clear as the water gathered and drained away. Bullrushes shot up beside the watercourses, and suddenly there were waterfowl round about, erupting into flight as one approached. We saw the sky reflected in water for the first time. Stranger still, the whole countryside was green, a color we scarcely knew. Evidences of the fertility of the soil were all about us. Trees sprang up as the waters receded around our house, and before long a new clump of eucalyptus saplings was well launched in life. On walks we would find enormous mushrooms, as large as a dinner plate, but perfectly formed. These we would gather to take home to grill on top of the wood stove, filling the house with a wonderful aroma. Walks became adventures of a new kind because they were likely to reveal some new plant or flower not

aboriginal from the aborigines, the native people of Australia
weatherboard siding
ubiquitous found everywhere
corrugated folded into ridges and grooves

bush wide-open lands in Australia with very few people
mitigate lessen the effect of
waft float on breeze
watercourses paths of water
aroma gentle scent

seen before, or show us why the aboriginal ovens were located where they were, close to what was once a stream or a water hole. We made a wooden raft and poled it cheerfully around the lake near the house, alighting on islands that were old sandhills, now suddenly sprouting grass.

Everywhere one went on the property was a vision of plenty. Dams brimmed with water. Sheep and cattle bloomed with health and nourishment. It was clear that there would be an abundant crop of wool, whiter and longer than any we had ever grown. On the heavier land, tall strong grasses grew resembling the pampas grass of Argentina. My father looked at it dubiously. When it dried it would be a fire hazard, and so a fresh herd of cattle was bought to eat it down and fatten for the market. Best of all, my father planned a late lambing season that year, and the young lambs, nourished by their mother's ample milk, frisked away like creatures in a child's picture book.

alighting   landing on
pampas grass   tall grass native to South America

dubiously   doubtfully

Think It Over

1. Why was water so important? How did its presence and absence affect this family's life?

2. Why do you think it was so amazing to Jill to see the sky reflected in water? What are some natural features you have never seen? What might it be like to experience one of these features?

ANCIENT EGYPT

In Her Own Words

by Hatshepsut, Queen of Egypt c. 1500 B.C.

Around 1500 B.C. young Hatshepsut became Queen of Egypt. When her husband, the king, died, Hatshepsut began to rule for her son, the prince and heir. Instead of turning over the throne to him, Hatshepsut made herself pharaoh. She ruled Egypt for more than twenty years. Here, she describes her right to the Egyptian throne.

> Now my heart turns to and fro,
> In thinking what will the people say,
> They who shall see my monument in after years,
> And shall speak of what I have done.
>
> No one rebels against me in all lands.
> He* gave it to him who came from him,
> Knowing I would rule it for him.
> I am his daughter in very truth,
> Who serves him, who knows what he ordains.

The Egyptian god Amun.

> My command stands firm like the mountains and
> the sun's disk shines and spreads rays over the
> titulary of my august person, and my falcon rises
> high above the kingly banner unto all eternity.

ordain   order

ANCIENT EGYPT

In Her Own Words

by Ankhesenpaton, Queen of Egypt c. 1350 B.C.

Queen Ankhesenpaton's husband, the legendary Tutankhamen, also died while ruling Egypt. They had no sons. Unlike Hatshepsut, Ankhesenpaton chose to find a new king by joining forces with another kingdom. Here, she asks that king for one of his sons to become her new husband and King of Egypt.

> My husband, Nib-khuruia,* has recently died, and I have no
> son. But thy sons, they say, are many. If thou wilt send me a son
> of thine, he shall become my husband.

Official name of Tutankhamen, who ruled c. 1379–1362 B.C.

Think It Over

1. Who are the people Hatshepsut refers to?

2. Why do you think Hatshepsut decided to make herself pharaoh? What do her historic words tell you about her decision?

3. How did each queen try to solve the problems created by a king's death? Which solution do you think might work best? Which one would you use? Why?

ISRAEL/EGYPT
"Moses and the Ten Commandments"

Moses was a prophet recognized by Jews, Christians, and Muslims. He is thought to have lived in the 1200s B.C. According to the Old Testament, Moses went up a mountain to speak with God. God told Moses ten rules of good behavior and ordered Moses to share these with the people. These rules, known as the Ten Commandments, form the basis of many modern religions.

Moses led the people out of the camp to meet God. Fearfully, they stationed themselves at the foot of the mountain. Alone, Moses went up. Then from the top of the mountain, God said:

"I, the Lord, am your God.

"You shall not have other gods besides me, nor shall you worship them. For I, the Lord your God, am a jealous God, punishing those who hate me, but showing mercy to those who love me and keep my commandments.

"You shall not take the name of the Lord, your God, in vain.

"Remember to keep holy the Sabbath Day. Six days you may labor, but on the seventh, no work may be done.

"Honor your father and your mother, that you may have a long life.

"You shall not kill.

"You shall not commit impure acts.

"You shall not steal.

"You shall not bear false witness against your neighbor.

"You shall not covet your neighbor's wife.

"You shall not covet your neighbor's house or any other thing that belongs to him."

All the people solemnly promised to obey these Ten Commandments of the Lord. "We will do everything that the Lord has told us!" they exclaimed.

stationed   placed themselves in waiting

covet   wish to have

Think It Over

1. Why do you think the Ten Commandments are meaningful to many different religious groups?

PERSIA

"The King's Wealth"

from *Babylon, Next to Nineveh* by Edward Rice

When Harun al-Rashid died in 809, his son Muhammad al-Amin ordered an inventory of the khalif's belongings. The secretaries and storekeepers spent four months inspecting and counting the treasures. To show the kind of things a khalif might possess, and to give an idea of his wealth, here is the inventory.

4,000	embroidered robes
4,000	silk cloaks lined with sable, mink, and other furs
10,000	shifts and shirts
10,000	caftans
2,000	underdrawers of various kinds
4,000	turbans
1,000	hoods
1,000	capes of various types
5,000	kerchiefs
500	pieces of velvet
100,000	mithqals [a mithqal equaled about 4.25 grams] of musk
100,000	mithqals of ambergris
1,000	baskets of Indian aloes
1,000	precious china vessels, many kinds of perfumes, gems valued by the jewelers at four million dinars [a dinar was worth about ten dollars]
500,000	dinars
1,000	jeweled rings
1,000	Armenian carpets
4,000	curtains
5,000	cushions
5,000	pillows
1,500	silk carpets
100	silk rugs
1,000	silk cushions and pillows
300	Maysani carpets
1,000	Darabjirdi carpets
1,000	cushions with silk brocade

1,000	inscribed silk cushions
1,000	silk curtains
300	silk brocade curtains
500	Tabari carpets
1,000	Tabari cushions
1,000	pillows (mirfada type)
1,000	pillows (mikhadda type)
1,000	ewers
300	stoves
1,000	candlesticks
2,000	brass objects of various kinds
1,000	belts
10,000	decorated swords
50,000	swords for the guards and the pages
150,000	lances
100,000	bows
1,000	special suits of armor
50,000	common suits of armor
10,000	helmets
20,000	breastplates
150,000	shields
4,000	special saddles
30,000	common saddles
4,000	pairs of half-boots, most lined with sable, mink, and other kinds of fur, with a knife and a kerchief in each half-boot
4,000	pairs of socks
4,000	small tents with their appurtenances
150	marquees

Harun al-Rashid   supreme ruler of Baghdad, the center of the Persian Empire, from A.D. 786–809
inventory   list
khalif   supreme ruler
sable, mink   small, furry animals with very valuable fur
underdrawer   underwear
turban   head covering made by wrapping cloth
musk   a strongly scented substance made from musk deer

ambergris   a waxy substance coming from whales, used in making perfume
ewer   pitcher
lance   a weapon similar to a spear
appurtenance   accessory, extra part
marquee   large tent

Think It Over

1. What are some adjectives you might use to describe the court of Harun al-Rashid?

2. Why might a khalif need all these possessions? How do you think Harun al-Rashid used them?

Speech
★★★★★

BYZANTIUM

Women Leaders Take a Stand
by Byzantine Empress Theodora

In the year 532, the empire of Empress Theodora and
her husband Emperor Justinian was under attack by
rebels. When Justinian wanted to escape to safety,
Theodora made this passionate speech to stop him.

My lords, the present occasion is too serious to allow me to follow the convention that a woman should not speak in a man's
council. Those whose interests are threatened by extreme danger
should think only of the wisest course of action, not of conventions.

In my opinion, flight is not the right course, even if it should
bring us to safety. It is impossible for a person, having been
born into this world, not to die; but for one who has reigned it
is intolerable to be a fugitive. May I never be deprived of this
purple robe, and may I never see the day when those who meet
me do not call me empress.

If you wish to save yourself, my lord, there is no difficulty. We
are rich; over there is the sea, and yonder are the ships. Yet re-
flect for a moment whether, when you have once escaped to a
place of security, you would not gladly exchange such safety for
death. As for me, I agree with the adage that the royal purple is
the noblest shroud.

convention   commonly accepted practice but not an
  actual law
reigned   ruled, been a monarch
intolerable   impossible to stand
fugitive   one who runs away and is followed

purple robe   purple is a color associated with royalty
yonder   over there
adage   old saying
shroud   a cloth wrapped around a corpse before burial

Think It Over

1. How does Empress Theodora's speech make you feel? Do you agree or
   disagree with her position? What are your reasons?

2. What does the empress mean when she says "may I never see the day
   when those who meet me do not call me empress"?

Literature

ANCIENT GREECE

A Spartan Reply
retold by Louis Untermeyer

Sparta was one of the great Greek city-states. These cities were self-contained, with their own governments. Each had its own personality—Sparta being known for its army and its simple and disciplined style of life.

King Philip of Macedon, father of Alexander the Great, had won so many victories and had captured so much territory that everyone expected him to invade Greece. This he planned to do, but he hesitated because of the Spartans.

The Spartans lived in that part of Greece known as Laconia. A brave and simple people, utterly fearless, they were not given to boasting or vain talk. They used few words and chose those words carefully; their sentences were so short that they were called "laconic," a form of speech native to Laconia.

Philip at last decided that he would wait no longer. Assembling a vast army, he brought it to the borders of Laconia. Then he sent a message to the Spartans.

"When I invade your country," he warned them, "if you do not yield at once, I will burn your villages and destroy your cities. If I enter Laconia I will level it to the ground."

The Spartans did not waste words or time. Their answer came back immediately, a truly laconic reply. It consisted of a single word.

The word was "IF!"

Macedon   country within ancient Greece
Alexander the Great   ruler who expanded his father's earlier conquests to rule a huge empire in Greece, Persia, and briefly, India
yield   give way, surrender

Think It Over

1. What do you think the Spartans were trying to say with their reply?

2. Today, a person who owns very little is sometimes referred to as spartan. What do you think this means?

ANCIENT GREECE
"Storm in the State"
by Alcaéus of Mytiléne

Big changes in your life can make you feel like you are caught in the middle of a storm. Poets have long used nature to describe human events such as wars and political struggles. Alcaéus of Mytiléne was a Greek nobleman. He was very involved in politics, sometimes fighting for change and sometimes fighting against it. Perhaps his poem comments on these changes.

I cannot understand how the winds are set
against each other. Now from this side and now
   from that the waves roll. We between them
     run with the wind in our black ship driven,

hard pressed and laboring under the giant storm.
All round the mast-step washes the sea we shipped.
   You can see through the sail already
     where there are opening rents within it.

The forestays slacken. . . .

mast-step   raised platform from which the mast of the ship rises
rents   tears
forestays   rope securing the forward mast to the ship's deck
slacken   weaken, lose their tension

Think It Over

1. What do you think Alcaéus is describing? What are some images he uses to paint his word picture?

2. If Alcaéus' ship is a symbol of the society in which he lived, what is happening to that society?

Name _____ Date _____

THE ROMAN EMPIRE

For about two hundred years after the reign of Augustus Caesar (27 B.C.-A.D. 14) the Roman Empire thrived. This period is known as the Pax Romana, or Roman peace. By about A.D. 400, however, the Empire was divided and weakened. In A.D. 410, the city of Rome itself was invaded and conquered by the Visigoths, who were from what is now Germany. These eyewitness accounts take you back to Rome in its glory and its defeat.

"Pliny the Younger"
from Pliny: *Letters and Panegyricus*, translated by Betty Radice

The typical wealthy Roman of the *Pax Romana* period might live in a villa such as this one.

The villa is large enough for all requirements, and is not expensive to keep in repair. At its entrance there is a modest . . . hall; then come the cloisters [covered walkways], which are rounded into the likeness of the letter D, and these enclose a smallish but handsome courtyard. . . . Facing the middle of the cloisters is a cheerful inner court, then comes a dining-room running down toward the shore . . . and when the sea is disturbed by the southwest wind the room is just flecked by the spray of the spent waves. There are folding doors on all sides of it . . . [and] at the back one can see through the inner court, the cloisters, the courtyard . . . and through them the woods and the distant hills. . . . Adjoining one of the rooms is a chamber with one wall rounded like a bay. . . . In the wall of this room I have had shelves placed like a library, which contains the volumes I not only read, but read over and over again. Next to it is a sleeping chamber. . . . Close by is the tennis court, which receives the warmest rays of the afternoon sun: on one side a tower has been built with two sitting rooms on the ground-floor commanding [a view of] a wide expanse of the sea. . . . There is also a second tower. . . . It looks out upon an exercise ground, which runs round the garden."

"Seneca"
from *The World of Rome* by Michael Greant

One of the favorite activities of ancient Romans was watching combat games. These fights were between men or between men and animals. Most fights were to the death, and the crowd was thrilled by the violence.

I've happened to drop in upon the midday entertainment of the arena in hope of . . . a touch of relief in which men's eyes may find rest after a glut of human blood. No, no: far from it. . . . Now for butchery plain and simple! The combatants have nothing to protect them: their bodies are utterly open to every blow: never a thrust but finds its mark. . . . What good is armor? What good is swordsmanship? All these things only put off death a little. In the morning men are matched with lions and bears. . . . Death is the fighter's only exit.

Seneca then records some of the crowd's remarks, making the point that the spectators were more bloodthirsty than the fighters.

glut   overflow, too much
combatants   those fighting

"Aelius Aristides"
from *The Romans* by R. H. Barrow

A Greek writer, Aelius Aristides, described the benefits of the glorious Pax Romana as though he was speaking to it.

Only those, if there are any, who are outside your Empire are to be pitied for the blessings they are denied. Better than all others you have demonstrated the universal saying, that the earth is the mother of all and the common fatherland of all. Greek and barbarian [non-Greek], with his property or without it, can go with ease wherever he likes, just as though going from one homeland to another. . . . You have measured the whole world, spanned rivers with bridges . . . cut through mountains to make level roads for traffic . . . filled desolate places with farmsteads, and made life easier by supplying its necessities amid law and order. Everywhere are gymnasia, fountains, gateways, temples, factories, schools. . . . Cities are radiant in their splendor and their grace, and the whole earth is as trim as a garden.

barbarian   non-Greek
desolate   wild and unsettled
amid   in the middle of
gymnasia   exercise centers

"Saint Jerome"

from *A Treasury of the World's Great Letters*,
edited and compiled by M. Lincoln Schuster

Saint Jerome made his mark on history by translating the Old Testament Bible from He-brew to Latin. In his time, most people knew Latin, so the translation brought the Bible's words to the people. Toward the end of his life, he was saddened to see the Roman Empire fall, as he wrote in this letter to his friends.

Indeed, the Roman world is falling; yet we still hold up our heads instead of bowing them. The East, indeed, seemed to be free from these perils; but now, in the year just past, the wolves of the North have been let loose from their remotest fastnesses, and have overrun great provinces. They have laid siege to Antioch, and invested cities that were once the capitals of no mean states.

*Non mihi si linguae centum sint oraque
    centum,
Ferrea vox, omnes scelerum comprendere
    formas,
Omnia poenarum percurrere nomine possim.* *

(*Had I a hundred tongues, a hundred
    mouths,
A voice of iron, I could not compass all
Their crimes, nor tell their penalties by
    name.
                    —Virgil, Aeneid VI, 625–627)

Well may we be unhappy, for it is our sins that have made the barbarians strong; as in the days of Hezekiah, so today is God using the fury of the barbarian to execute His fierce anger. Rome's army, once the lord of the world, trembles today at sight of the foe.

Who will hereafter believe that Rome has to fight now within her own borders, not for glory but for life? and, as the poet Lucan says, "If Rome be weak, where shall strength be found?"

And now a dreadful rumor has come to hand. Rome has been besieged, and its citizens have been forced to buy off their lives with gold. My voice cleaves to my throat; sobs choke my utterance. The city which had taken the whole world captive is itself taken. Famine too has done its awful work.

The world sinks into ruin; all things are perishing save our sins; these alone flourish. The great city is swallowed up in one vast conflagration; everywhere Romans are in exile.

Who could believe it? who could believe that Rome, built up through the ages by the conquest of the world, had fallen; that the mother of nations had become their tomb? who could imagine that the proud city, with its careless security and its boundless wealth, is brought so low that her children are outcasts and beggars? We cannot indeed help them; all we can do is sympathize with them, and mingle our tears with theirs.

---

peril danger
wolves of the North barbarian groups from northern
    Europe
laid siege attacked
invested taken over
mean small

Hezekiah king of Judah from the 700s B.C. whose
    kingdom was invaded
besieged attacked
cleaves clings to, will not leave
utterance speech, sounds
conflagration huge fire

Think It Over

1. Why do you think the Romans so enjoyed watching physical combat? Think about how the Empire had established itself.

2. What characteristics do you think Pliny the Younger valued in his surroundings?

3. How did Rome change from the time of Aelius Aristedes to the time of Saint Jerome?

Name _____ Date _____

Royal Letters
between The Emperor of Rome and the Queen of Palmyra

Lucius Domitius Aurelianus, "Restorer of the Roman Empire" in the third century after Christ, began his military career as a common soldier. After attaining the highest command in the army, he was elected Emperor in 270. A sweep of continued conquests, almost world-wide in scope, was temporarily halted when Zenobia, Queen of Palmyra, held Syria, Asia Minor, and Egypt against him. In the following letter, the Emperor lays down his terms:

What I now require you ought to have done long since of your own accord. I command you to surrender the city, and thereupon promise both you and yours your lives, but not your liberty. You, Zenobia, and your children must be content to go where I and the most august Senate of Rome think fit to place you. Your jewels, gold, silver, and other riches must all be confiscated to the Roman treasury. Your subjects alone will be freed from captivity, and have their privileges assured them.

The Queen, however, was not afraid to hurl back her own defiance. She had helped her late husband in a victorious war against Persia and had inherited and effectively exercised a virtual sovereignty over the Near East. Moreover, she was a learned woman, instructed by the great Longinus in the arts and sciences, and a master of Latin, Greek, Coptic, and Syrian. Her reply to Aurelian follows:

No man ever yet presumed to command me as you have done. Bravery alone, Aurelian, will accomplish your ends in war. You demand that I surrender my city of Palmyra as if you did not know that my ancestress, Cleopatra, preferred to die a queen than live a slave, of however great position, to your predecessor Augustus.

We await help from the Persians. The Saracens arm for us; the Armenians have declared in our favor; a band of highwaymen has defeated your army in Syria. Then judge what is in store for you when all these forces arrive. You will surely change your tone then, and not command me so imperiously to give up my birthright, as if you were the absolute disposer of the universe.

attaining achieving
accord willingly, without being asked
august respected
confiscated taken from
subjects the people under a monarch's rule
sovereignty rule as monarch
learned educated
Coptic language of the Copts, an ancient Egyptian people

ancestress female ancestor
predecessor one who comes before
imperiously as if one has a great deal of power
birthright that which a person has or receives simply because of who or where he or she is born
disposer ruler

Think It Over

1. How would you describe Zenobia's character? Was she brave or foolish to take the position she took? Why do you think so?

2. What do you think Aurelian was telling Zenobia in his letter? What did he plan to do?

The Words of Queen Theodora Boadicea

from *Biography of Distinguished Women* by Sarah Josepha Hale

In the first century A.D., the Roman Empire still controlled what is now England. Queen Boadicea led her people in rebelling against that Roman rule.

It will not be the first time, Britons, that you have been victorious under the conduct of your queen. For my part, I come not here as one descended of royal blood, not to fight for empire or riches, but as one of the common people, to avenge the loss of their liberty, the wrongs of myself and children.

Is it not much better to fall honourably in defence of liberty, than be again exposed to the outrages of the Romans? Such, at least, is my resolution; as for you men, you may, if you please, live and be slaves!

Britons   people in what is now England
victorious   having won the battle or war
conduct   actions, leadership
avenge   get revenge for, repay
wrongs   damage or injury done
outrages   attacks against people and property

Think It Over

1. What did Boadicea say she was fighting for?

2. Why do you think Boadicea said she was addressing the Britons "as one of the common people"?

CREDITS

page 114 Excerpt from *Maroo of the Winter Caves.* Copyright © 1984 by Ann Turnbull. Reprinted by permission of Clarion Books/Houghton Mifflin Company. All rights reserved.

page 117 Excerpts from *Napoleon's Russian Campaign* by Philippe-Paul de Segur, translated by J. David Townsend. Copyright © 1958 by J. David Townsend.

page 119–120 Quoted from *A Treasury of the World's Great Letters*, edited and compiled by M. Lincoln Schuster. Copyright © 1940 by Simon & Schuster, Inc. Copyright renewed 1968 by Simon & Schuster, Inc.

page 120 Elaine Feinstein, *Marina Tsvetavera,* (1989).

page 121 From *Open Letters* by Vaclav Havel. Copyright © 1991 by Vaclav Havel, published by Alfred A. Knopf, Inc.

page 122 From *The Endless Steppe* by Esther Hautzig. Copyright © 1968 by Esther Hautzig, published by HarperKeypoint, an imprint of HarperCollins Publishers.

page 123 From *Mokhtar of the Atlas Mountains* by Elisabeth Thiebaut, translated by Bridget Daly. First published by Librairie Larousse, France, 1983. English translation Copyright © 1984 by Macdonald & Co. (Publishers) Ltd., England.

page 125 Quoted in *Lend Me Your Ears: Great Speeches in History,* selected by William Safire. Copyright © 1992 by the Cobbett Corporation, published by W. W. Norton and Company.

page 128 Excerpt from "A Handful of Dates" by Tayeb Salih. From *The Wedding of Zein,* published by Heinemann Educational Books, London.

page 130 Interview with Congolese villagers, 1893, from the report on conditions in the Africa Free State by British consul Roger Casement. Quoted in *Africa: The Struggle for Independence* by Dennis Wepman. Copyright © 1993 by Dennis Wepman, published by Facts on File, Inc.

page 131 Kwame Nkrumah, Ghana, address to the General Assembly of the United Nations, 1961, quoted by David Rooney, *Kwame Nkrumah* (New York: St. Martin's Press, 1988).

page 132 From *Hope and Suffering: Sermons and Speeches of Desmond Mpilo Tutu,* compiled by Mothobi Mutloatse, edited by John Webster. Published by W. B. Eermans, 1983.

page 132 Desmond Tutu to a group of black villagers, as quoted in *Desmond Tutu* by David Winner. Gareth Stevens Publishing, 1989.

page 132 Desmond Tutu, in his letter to Prime Minister John Vorster, as quoted in *Desmond Tutu* by David Winner. Gareth Stevens Publishing, 1989.

page 134–135 From *The Royal Kingdoms of Ghana, Mali, and Songhay* by Patricia and Fredrick McKissack, Copyright © 1994 by Patricia and Fredrick McKissack. Reprinted by permission of Henry Holt & Co., Inc.

page 136 Copyright © 1973 by John Nagenda. Selection from *Mukasa,* first published by Macmillan.

page 139 From *The Dhammapada* pp. 88–90, 94, 96, 121, 133, 148–49, translated by Eknath Easwaran, Copyright © 1986, Niligri Press, Tomales, CA.

page 140 *Savitri: A Tale of Ancient India* by Aaron Shepard. Text Copyright © 1992 by Aaron Shepard. Used with permission of Albert Whitman & Co.

page 143 By the Shan People of Southern Annam. From *Contes Tjames* by A. Landes, Saigon, 1887. Quoted in *I Saw a Rocket Walk a Mile* by Carl Withers. Copyright © 1965 by Carl Withers, published by Holt, Rinehart and Winston, Inc.

page 144 From *City Kids in China* by Peggy Thomson. Copyright © 1991 by Peggy Thomson, published by HarperCollins Publishers.

page 146 Excerpt from *The Year of Impossible Goodbyes.* Copyright © 1991 by Sook Nyul Choi. Reprinted by permission of Houghton Mifflin Company. All rights reserved.

page 148 "The Coconut Tree" from *Tales from the South Pacific Islands* by Anne Gittins. Copyright © 1977 by Anne Gittins, reprinted by permission of Stemmer House Publishers, Owings Mills, MD.

page 150 From *Dreamtime: Aboriginal Stories* by Oodgeroo. Copyright © 1972 by Oodgeroo Nunukul. By permission of Lothrop, Lee & Shepard Books, a division of William Morrow & Company, Inc.

page 152 From *The Road from Coorain* by Jill Ker Conway. Copyright © 1989 by Jill Ker Conway. Reprinted by permission of Alfred A. Knopf, Inc.

page 154 Quoted from her obelisk inscription in *Ancient Egyptian Literature, Volume II: The New Kingdom,* Miriam Lichtheim, ed. and tr., 1976.

page 154 Quoted in *The Remarkable Women of Ancient Egypt* by Barbara Lesko, 1978.

page 154 Letter to Shuppiluliuma, the Hittite king (62 B.C.), Quoted in *When Egypt Ruled the East,* Ch. 15, by George Steindorff and Keith C. Seele, 1942.

page 155 From *The Bible for Children,* written and illustrated by the Daughters of St. Paul. Copyright © 1968, 1977 by the Daughters of St. Paul. Published by the Daughters of St. Paul.

page 156 From *Babylon, Next to Nineveh* by Edward Rice. Copyright © 1979 by Edward Rice.

page 158 Quoted in *Lend Me Your Ears: Great Speeches in History,* selected by William Safire. Copyright © 1992 by the Cobbett Corporation, published by W.W. Norton and Company.

page 159 From *The World's Great Stories: Fifty-Five Legends that Live Forever* by Louis Untermeyer. Copyright © 1964 by Louis Untermeyer. Reprinted by permission of M. Evans and Company, Inc.

page 160 From *Greek Lyrics* by Richard Lattimore. Copyright © 1949, 1955, and 1960 by Richmond Lattimore. Reprinted by permission of the University of Chicago Press.

page 161 *Pliny: Letters and Panegyricus,* translated by Betty Radice. Cambridge, MA: Harvard University Press, 1969.

page 162 Seneca, *Epistulae morales.* Quoted in Michael Greant, *The World of Rome.* New York: New American Library, 1960.

page 162 Aelius Aristides, *Roman Panegyric.* Quoted in *The Romans* by R. H. Barrow. Baltimore: Penguin Books, 1949.

page 163 Quoted from *A Treasury of the World's Great Letters*, edited and compiled by M. Lincoln Schuster. Copyright © 1940 by Simon & Schuster, Inc. Copyright renewed 1968 by Simon & Schuster, Inc.

page 165 From *A Treasury of the World's Great Letters*, edited and compiled by M. Lincoln Schuster. Copyright © 1940 by Simon & Schuster, Inc. Copyright renewed 1968 by Simon & Schuster, Inc.

page 166 Quoted in *Biography of Distinguished Women* by Sarah Josepha Hale, 1876.

Note: Every effort has been made to locate the copyright owner of material used in this textbook. Omissions brought to our attention will be corrected in subsequent editions.